The Ripple Effect

The Ripple Effect

How Rhinos Impact Ecosystems Downstream

Rayan Musk

Spectra Enterprise

CONTENTS

INDEX

Introduction

INTRODUCTION

In the mind boggling embroidery of Earth's environments, each specie assumes an unmistakable part, adding to the sensitive equilibrium that supports life. Among the alluring megafauna that wander our planet, rhinos stand as both antiquated sentinels and contemporary images of nature. Past their impressive presence and dazzling charm, rhinos fill a significant environmental need, going about as engineers of scenes and impetuses for biodiversity. This paper leaves on a far reaching investigation of the far reaching influence made by rhinos in environments downstream. As we dig into the interconnected trap of connections that emanates from these great animals, we reveal the significant impact they apply on verdure, fauna, streams, and the complex dance of life that unfurls downstream.

1. **The Cornerstone Job of Rhinos in Earthly Environments**
1. **Environment Specialists:**
   Rhinos, containing a few animal types like the dark rhinoceros (Diceros bicornis) and the white rhinoceros (Ceratotherium simum), are not simple observers in their surroundings; they are biological system engineers forming the scenes they possess. Through their taking care of propensities, going from specific brushing to seed dispersal, rhinos shape the vegetation mosaic, impacting the design and structure of plant networks. This designing ability reaches out past their actual effect on the actual texture of biological systems.
2. **Seed Dispersal Elements:**
   As programs and nibblers, rhinos are instrumental in the dispersal of seeds across tremendous spans of living space. The seeds of the plants they consume frequently go through their gastrointestinal systems safe, profiting from an excursion that upgrades their possibilities of germination. The cooperative connection among rhinos and the plant realm is a demonstration of the complex dance of coevolution, where the endurance of the two players is complicatedly connected.

3. **Biodiversity Areas of interest:**

Rhino-impacted scenes arise as biodiversity areas of interest, holding onto a rich embroidery of plant species adjusted to their presence. The different exhibit of plants, from grasses to bushes, upholds an outpouring of life, giving food to various herbivores, bugs, and more modest warm blooded creatures. The presence of rhinos not just adds to the assortment of plant species yet in addition impacts the overflow and circulation of related fauna.

II. The Expanding influence in Herbivore Elements

1. **Herbivore People group Construction:**
   The environmental stage set by rhinos resounds through herbivore networks downstream. By modifying the accessibility of search and making assorted microhabitats, rhinos shape the elements of herbivore populaces. The mosaic of vegetation types made by their particular taking care of examples upholds a scope of herbivores with shifted dietary inclinations, encouraging an amicable concurrence.

2. **Rivalry and Specialty Dividing:**

Rhinos, as huge herbivores, share their living spaces with a horde of other nibblers and programs. The intricate interaction of rivalry and specialty apportioning unfurls as various herbivore species adjust to particular dietary specialties and taking care of procedures. Understanding these elements gives bits of knowledge into the complex connections that administer herbivore networks downstream from rhino-impacted environments.

III. Flowing Impacts on Meat eater Elements

1. **Hunter Prey Cooperations:**
   The far reaching influence started by rhinos stretches out to the higher classes of the food web, affecting the elements of carnivore populaces. The overflow and dispersion of herbivores, etched by rhino-prompted living space heterogeneity, assume a urgent part in forming hunter prey collaborations. Carnivores, from large felines to searching birds, find food in the mosaic of herbivore overflow made by rhino-designed scenes.

2. **Scrounger Societies and Flesh Environment:**

Rhinos, as strong herbivores, likewise add to the accessibility of remains, making a natural specialty for scroungers. The remains of rhinos, whether from regular mortality or predation, become central focuses for scrounger societies. The multifaceted snare of remains nature, from vultures to more modest scroungers, unfurls downstream as an outcome of the rhino's part in molding herbivore and hunter elements.

IV. Streams as Conductors of Impact

1. **Riparian Zones and Water Quality:**
   The effect of rhinos on biological systems reaches out past earthbound domains to the complex organization of streams. Riparian zones, impacted by rhino movement, assume a critical part in water quality and supplement cycling. Rhinos, through their floundering ways of behaving and particular taking care of along riverbanks, add to the enhancement of riparian vegetation, which, thus, impacts water quality downstream.

2. **Wetland Biological systems and Biodiversity Centers:**

Rhinos are frequently connected with wetland natural surroundings, using these biological systems for cooling, taking care of, and social communications. The impact of rhinos on wetlands changes these regions into biodiversity centers, supporting an abundance of sea-going and earthly species. The interconnectedness of rhino-impacted wetlands with downstream streams makes a unique framework where the presence of rhinos swells through the whole sea-going environment.

V. Human-Creature Communications in Rhino-Affected Scenes

1. **Human-Untamed life Struggle and Conjunction:**
   The presence of rhinos in scenes unavoidably crosses with human exercises, prompting complex elements of contention and conjunction. As rhinos shape the dissemination of herbivores and impact land use, experiences with nearby networks become unavoidable. Understanding the subtleties of human-untamed life cooperations downstream from rhino natural surroundings is significant for cultivating systems that offset preservation objectives with the prosperity of neighborhood populaces.

2. **Preservation Difficulties and Amazing open doors:**

The gradually expanding influence started by rhinos brings both protection difficulties and open doors. Human-untamed life struggle, poaching dangers, and environment debasement address difficulties that request key mediations. On the other side, the mind boggling environmental dance put into high gear by rhinos offers open doors for protectionists to use their biological significance in making feasible administration plans.

VI. The Worldwide Setting: Rhinos as Lead Species for Preservation

1. **Protection Meaning of Rhinos:**
   Past their restricted effects, rhinos arise as leader species for more extensive

preservation drives. The predicament of rhinos, confronting dangers like poaching and environment misfortune, catches worldwide consideration, filling in as an energizing point for more extensive biodiversity preservation. The appealling charm of rhinos can be saddled to advocate for environment protection, against poaching measures, and worldwide coordinated effort in shielding biological systems downstream.

2. **Transboundary Protection and Worldwide Coordinated effort:**

Rhino preservation frequently ranges public boundaries, requiring transboundary drives and worldwide coordinated effort. The interconnected idea of biological systems downstream from rhino natural surroundings highlights the requirement for deliberate endeavors past political limits. The worldwide local area's reaction to rhino protection reflects more extensive patterns in global participation for safeguarding biodiversity and moderating ecological difficulties.

1. **Definition of the Ripple Effect in Ecology**

The expression "expanding influence" holds a special reverberation in the domain of biology, bringing out pictures of interconnectedness and the extensive results of activities inside regular frameworks. In the unique dance of life on The planet, each organic entity, cooperation, and natural change can set off a progression of flowing impacts that reverberate across biological systems. This exposition dives into the meaning of the far reaching influence in biology, investigating its different signs, systems, and suggestions for the complex trap of life that characterizes our planet.

II. Characterizing the Far reaching influence in Nature

1. **Calculated System:**
   At its center, the far reaching influence in nature alludes to the successive and frequently roundabout outcomes of a bother or change in one piece of an environment. Similar to the concentric circles that emanate outward when a stone is tossed into a lake, the expanding influence appears as a progression of reactions that stretch out past the underlying focal point. This idea typifies the interconnected idea of natural frameworks, where no organic entity or ecological variable works in seclusion.

2. **Spatial and Worldly Elements:**
   The far reaching influence is intrinsically unique, displaying both spatial and worldly aspects. Spatially, the results of a biological aggravation can spread through different trophic levels, influencing various species and environments. Transiently, the impacts can unfurl over short or broadened periods, affecting environmental cycles, for example, populace elements, local area construction, and biological system working.

3. **Trophic Fountains and Collaborations:**

One of the quintessential signs of the expanding influence is seen in trophic fountains, where changes in the overflow or conduct of an animal varieties at one trophic level resound through numerous trophic levels. For instance, modifications in the number of inhabitants in top hunters can impact prey species, prompting a fountain of consequences for lower trophic levels and, at last, affecting plant networks.

III. Systems of the Expanding influence

1. **Immediate and Aberrant Pathways:**
   The expanding influence works through both immediate and circuitous pathways. Direct impacts happen when a bother straightforwardly impacts an animal varieties or natural element, setting off quick reactions. Backhanded impacts, then again, result from the flowing outcomes of an unsettling influence, frequently including different mediator connections and criticism circles.

2. **Species Associations:**
   Species cooperations, enveloping predation, contest, mutualism, and beneficial interaction, assume a urgent part in proliferating the far reaching influence. For example, the decay of a cornerstone animal categories can significantly affect the overflow and conveyance of different species inside the environment, setting off a chain response of biological results.

3. **Input Instruments:**
   Input instruments add to the intensification or hosing of the expanding influence. Positive input circles increase the underlying unsettling influence, prompting an acceleration of results. On the other hand, negative criticism circles go about as administrative systems, hosing the impacts and advancing strength inside the environment.

4. **Nonlinear Elements:**

The expanding influence frequently displays nonlinear elements, where little changes can set off lopsidedly enormous reactions. Nonlinearities in biological frameworks emerge from edge impacts, tipping focuses, and the interconnected idea of criticism circles. Understanding these nonlinear elements is fundamental for anticipating and dealing with the outcomes of natural annoyances.

IV. Instances of the Expanding influence in Environmental Frameworks

1. **Troop Elements in Savanna Biological systems**
   In savanna environments, the presence or nonappearance of enormous herbivores, for example, elephants can set off a gradually expanding influence with flowing outcomes. Elephants, through their searching and perusing ways of behaving, impact vegetation structure. Changes in vegetation influence the

overflow and dispersion of herbivores and, in this way, influence hunters and foragers. The far reaching influence, in this specific situation, highlights the reliance of species inside the savanna environment.

2. **Coral Reef Strength:**
Coral reefs give one more convincing illustration of the expanding influence in real life. Overfishing of herbivorous fish on coral reefs can prompt an excess of green growth, adversely affecting coral wellbeing. The downfall of coral reefs, thus, influences fish populaces and the vocations of networks reliant upon reef environments. This environmental gradually expanding influence features the weakness of interconnected marine frameworks.

3. **Environmental Change and Icy Biological systems:**

The continuous effects of environmental change on Icy biological systems represent a worldwide scale far reaching influence. Liquefying ocean ice modifies the environments of marine species, influencing the dissemination and overflow of prey for Cold hunters like polar bears. These changes, thusly, resound through the whole Icy food web, impacting the elements of species from tiny fish to dominant hunters.

V. Human-Prompted Gradually expanding influences:

1. **Land Use Change and Territory Fracture:**
Human exercises, especially land use change and living space fracture, can start gradually expanding influences with inescapable natural outcomes. The transformation of regular living spaces for horticulture or metropolitan improvement upsets environments, prompting the discontinuity of scenes. This fracture, thus, influences species versatility, hereditary variety, and biological system flexibility, making a gradually expanding influence that reaches out a long ways past the limits of modified scenes.

2. **Obtrusive Species Presentations:**

The presentation of obtrusive species is an exemplary illustration of a human-initiated expanding influence. Intrusive species can outcompete local verdure, upset supplement cycling, and change environment elements. The results reach out to local species populaces, biodiversity misfortune, and changes in biological system administrations, featuring the requirement for cautious administration to moderate the effects of obtrusive species.

VI. Suggestions for Protection and Environment The board

1. **Strength and Versatile Administration:**
Understanding the gradually expanding influence is fundamental for upgrading the versatility of biological systems and executing versatile administration methodologies. Tough environments can more readily endure unsettling influences

and recuperate from bothers. Versatile administration, informed by information on natural communications, permits preservationists and land chiefs to answer powerfully to changing circumstances and unanticipated results.

2. **Protection of Cornerstone Species:**
The protection of cornerstone species, which apply lopsided impact on environments, is a pivotal technique for relieving the unfortunate results of the gradually expanding influence. Safeguarding cornerstone species keeps up with biodiversity, balance out biological cycles, and improve the general flexibility of environments.

3. **Environment Availability and Hallway Protection:**

Saving biological system network through the protection of natural life passages is an essential way to deal with relieving the expanding influence of territory discontinuity. Halls work with the development of species, quality stream, and the trading of natural cycles between divided territories, advancing the general wellbeing and manageability of biological systems.

VII. Difficulties and Future Headings

1. **Intricacy and Vulnerability:**
The intricacy of environmental frameworks and the heap collaborations that add to the expanding influence present difficulties for anticipating and overseeing results. Vulnerabilities in environmental reactions to bothers highlight the requirement for continuous examination, checking, and versatile ways to deal with biological system the executives.

2. **Worldwide Change and Anthropogenic Effects:**

Anthropogenic effects, including environmental change, territory obliteration, and contamination, acquaint remarkable difficulties with biological systems. The worldwide idea of these difficulties underlines the significance of global cooperation, interdisciplinary examination, and creative protection systems to address the intricate and interconnected far reaching influences of human-instigated changes.

B. Importance of Understanding Ecosystem Interconnections
The regular world works as a finely tuned ensemble, where each note, regardless of how unobtrusive, adds to the congruity of life. At the core of this biological ensemble lies the idea of environment interconnections — the multifaceted snare of connections that tight spot species, living spaces, and ecological cycles together. This article investigates the significant significance of understanding environment interconnections, revealing insight into the heap manners by which these connections shape the wellbeing, strength, and manageability of our planet's biological systems.

II. The Snare of Life: Biological system Interconnections Characterized

1. **Characterizing Environment Interconnections:**
   Biological system interconnections, otherwise called natural reliance, allude to the unique connections and cooperations among the living life forms, their territories, and the physical and synthetic parts of their surroundings. This idea exemplifies that no component of an environment works in disconnection; rather, every part is complicatedly connected to other people, making a snare of relationship that supports life.
2. **Comprehensive Biological system View:**

Understanding biological system interconnections requires taking on an all encompassing perspective on environments. Rather than review individual species or parts in seclusion, this approach perceives that the soundness of a biological system is dependent upon the wellbeing of its interconnected parts. From the tiny communications in soil to the enormous scope movements of notable species, the snare of life is woven through endless interconnections.

III. Biodiversity as the Foundation of Interconnections

1. **Biodiversity's Job:**
   Biodiversity, the assortment of life on The planet, arises as a foundation of biological system interconnections. The huge number of species, each adjusted to explicit specialties and jobs, frames the structure blocks of working environments. The variety of life improves the magnificence of our planet as well as adds to the strength, efficiency, and versatility of environments.
2. **Cornerstone Species and Trophic Fountains:**

Inside the complex embroidered artwork of biodiversity, certain species assume outsized parts in forming biological system elements. Cornerstone species, for instance, excessively affect their environments. Their presence or nonappearance can set off trophic fountains — flowing impacts through various trophic levels — that resound across whole scenes, exhibiting the interconnectedness of species inside biological systems.

IV. Biological system Administrations: Supporting Human Prosperity

1. **Characterizing Environment Administrations:**
   Environments give a heap of administrations fundamental for human prosperity, all things considered known as biological system administrations. These administrations range from provisioning administrations, like food and water, to controlling administrations like environment guideline and fertilization, supporting administrations like soil arrangement, and social administrations that add to human prosperity and social character.

2. **Fertilization and Rural Efficiency:**
Environment interconnections, especially those including pollinators like honey bees and butterflies, assume a basic part in horticulture. The fertilization of harvests by these species upgrades rural efficiency, guaranteeing the overflow of organic products, vegetables, and nuts. The decay of pollinator populaces highlights the weakness of these interconnections and the possible repercussions for food security.

3. **Water Decontamination and Wetland Biological systems:**
Wetland environments act as normal water purifiers, sifting and detoxifying water through complex interconnections including plants, microorganisms, and actual cycles. The significance of wetlands in keeping up with water quality stretches out past their limits, affecting downstream biological systems and the networks that rely upon clean water sources.

4. **Environment Guideline and Woods Biological systems:**

Woods, going about as worldwide carbon sinks, assume a pivotal part in environment guideline. The interconnections inside woods biological systems, including the many-sided connections between trees, soil, and microorganisms, add to carbon sequestration. Understanding these interconnections is central for compelling environmental change moderation and variation.

V. Strength Notwithstanding Change

1. **Versatility Characterized:**
Biological system interconnections contribute essentially to the versatility of environments — their capacity to endure and recuperate from aggravations. Versatile environments can adjust to evolving conditions, ingest stuns, and keep up with their fundamental capabilities. The variety of species and the complicated snare of associations inside biological systems are key components that support their versatility.

2. **Biodiversity and Steadiness:**
Biodiversity is firmly connected to biological system strength and flexibility. Different biological systems, with various species and hereditary variety, are much of the time more steady despite ecological vacillations. The overt repetitiveness and complementarity of species inside biological systems add to their capacity to retain and recuperate from aggravations.

3. **Cross-Scale Versatility:**

Biological systems work at various scales, from neighborhood natural surroundings to provincial scenes. Understanding environment interconnections across these scales is indispensable for encouraging cross-scale versatility. The capacity of a nearby environment to recuperate from an aggravation might be impacted by processes happening at bigger scopes, featuring the requirement for an extensive comprehension of interconnections.

VI. Dangers to Biological system Interconnections

1. **Human-Incited Unsettling influences:**
   Human exercises, including deforestation, territory obliteration, contamination, and environmental change, present huge dangers to biological system interconnections. These aggravations can upset the fragile equilibrium of associations inside environments, prompting the disentangling of fundamental connections. As human effects strengthen, protecting environment interconnections becomes vital for moderating biodiversity misfortune and keeping up with biological equilibrium.

2. **Obtrusive Species and Adjusted Associations:**

The presentation of obtrusive species addresses a significant test to biological system interconnections. Intrusive species can outcompete local species, modify trophic communications, and upset supplement cycling. Understanding and dealing with these connections are urgent for forestalling the adverse results of intrusive species on local biodiversity and environment working.

VII. Protection Suggestions

1. **Safeguarding Territory Availability:**
   Protection techniques should focus on the conservation of natural surroundings network to keep up with biological system interconnections. Planning and safeguarding natural life passages that permit species to move between divided living spaces is fundamental for quality stream, populace feasibility, and the trading of environmental cycles.

2. **Rebuilding Nature:**
   Rebuilding nature, zeroed in on the reestablishment and recovery of corrupted biological systems, depends on a comprehension of environment interconnections. Reclamation endeavors that consider the mind boggling trap of connections inside biological systems are bound to prevail with regards to restoring practical and strong scenes.

3. **Environment Strong Protection:**

As environmental change presents new difficulties to biological systems, preservation endeavors should take on environment strong procedures. This includes understanding how changing climatic circumstances might adjust species dispersions, disturb movement examples, and impact biological cycles. Environment tough preservation embraces versatile administration and expects the likely changes in biological system interconnections.

VIII. Instructive Effort and Public Mindfulness

1. **Advancing Environmental Education:**
   Instructive effort and public mindfulness assume crucial parts in encouraging a comprehension of biological system interconnections. Advancing environmental proficiency engages people to see the value in the perplexing connections inside biological systems and perceive the results of human activities on these interconnections. Informed residents are bound to help protection drives and feasible practices.

2. **Resident Science Drives:**
   Drawing in the general population in resident science drives gives a road to people to contribute straightforwardly to the comprehension of biological system interconnections. Resident researchers can partake in checking biodiversity, following species relocations, and gathering information that add to logical examination and preservation endeavors.

3. **Overview of Rhinos and their Ecological Significance**

Rhinos, with their ancient heredity and notorious presence, stand as both grand creatures and essential supporters of the complex embroidered artwork of Earth's environments. This paper gives a thorough outline of rhinos, investigating their different species, transformative history, and the critical natural jobs they play in molding scenes and cultivating biodiversity.

II. Scientific categorization and Variety of Rhinos

1. **Rhino Species:**
   There are five surviving types of rhinoceros, each having particular attributes and possessing explicit districts of the world:
   White Rhinoceros (Ceratotherium simum): Found in Southern Africa, the white rhinoceros is described by its expansive mouth adjusted for eating on grasses.
   Dark Rhinoceros (Diceros bicornis): Local to different districts of Africa, the dark rhinoceros is known for its snared upper lip, appropriate for perusing on bushes and trees.
   Indian Rhinoceros (Rhinoceros unicornis): Possessing the Indian subcontinent, the Indian rhinoceros has a solitary horn and thick, reinforcement like skin.
   Sumatran Rhinoceros (Dicerorhinus sumatrensis): Found in Southeast Asia, the Sumatran rhinoceros is the littlest rhino species and has unmistakable hair on its body.
   Javan Rhinoceros (Rhinoceros sondaicus): Local to Java, Indonesia, the

Javan rhinoceros is basically imperiled, with a little populace in Ujung Kulon Public Park.

2. **Developmental History:**

Rhinos have a long and celebrated developmental history that goes back great many years. Fossil proof recommends that rhinoceros predecessors wandered the Earth during the Eocene age, developing into assorted structures over the long haul. The cutting edge rhino species we perceive today are the aftereffect of this developmental excursion, adjusted to various living spaces and biological specialties.

III. Biological Jobs of Rhinos

1. **Biological system Specialists:**
   Rhinos are perceived as cornerstone species and biological system engineers, applying a significant effect on the construction and capability of the scenes they possess. Their environmental jobs stretch out past being simple herbivores, as their taking care of and development designs shape biological systems in more ways than one.

2. **Vegetation The executives:**
   Rhinos assume a vital part in overseeing vegetation through their taking care of propensities. White rhinoceros, with their inclination for grasses, add to keeping up with open prairies. Dark rhinoceros, then again, peruse on bushes and trees, affecting the organization and design of plant networks. This specific herbivory makes a mosaic of environments, cultivating biodiversity.

3. **Seed Dispersal:**
   The stomach related cycles of rhinos are unpredictably connected to the dispersal of seeds. As they brush or peruse, rhinos consume an assortment of plant material, and the seeds frequently go through their gastrointestinal systems safe. This interaction upgrades seed germination and dispersal, adding to the recovery of plant species across scenes.

4. **Making Water Openings:**

Rhinos are known to make flounders, discouragements in the ground loaded up with water, through their floundering ways of behaving. These water openings act as urgent assets, for rhinos themselves as well as for a horde of different animal varieties. The presence of rhino-made water openings upgrades water accessibility, supporting a different exhibit of natural life in frequently parched or semi-dry living spaces.

IV. Communications with Different Species

1. **Herbivore Elements:**
   Rhinos impact the elements of herbivore networks in their living spaces. The mosaic of vegetation made by their taking care of examples upholds various

herbivores with various dietary inclinations. By molding the overflow and dissemination of herbivores, rhinos add to the many-sided equilibrium of species cooperations inside environments.

2. **Carnivore Elements:**
The presence of rhinos impacts carnivore elements through trophic cooperations. Enormous hunters, like lions and hyenas, may profit from the overflow of herbivores in rhino-affected scenes. Moreover, scroungers depend on rhino remains, adding to the carcass biology of the environment.

3. **Birds and Bugs:**

Rhinos draw in various birds and bugs that structure harmonious associations with them. Oxpeckers, for example, are known to benefit from ticks and different parasites tracked down on the skin of rhinos, giving a mutualistic administration. Bugs, drawn to rhino fertilizer, assume a part in supplement cycling and deterioration.

V. Protection Difficulties and Dangers

1. **Poaching for Horns:**
One of the most squeezing dangers to rhino populaces is poaching for their horns. Rhino horns, made out of keratin, have been dishonestly ascribed with restorative properties in some conventional Asian medication rehearses. This request has energized a worthwhile unlawful exchange, prompting a staggering decrease in rhino populaces, especially for the African species.

2. **Natural surroundings Misfortune and Fracture:**
Natural surroundings misfortune and fracture present critical difficulties to rhino preservation. As human populaces grow and infringe upon regular environments, rhinos face the deficiency of basic taking care of and favorable places. Territory discontinuity upsets environmental cycles, impedes rhino development, and adds to hereditary seclusion.

3. **Human-Natural life Struggle:**

The extension of human exercises into rhino territories improves the probability of human-untamed life struggle. Rhinos, especially when they adventure into farming regions, may experience neighborhood networks, prompting clashes that endanger both human jobs and rhino endurance. Creating techniques for conjunction is fundamental for alleviating these contentions.

VI. Preservation Drives and Examples of overcoming adversity

1. **Hostile to Poaching Endeavors:**
Preservation associations and state run administrations have executed thorough enemy of poaching measures to safeguard rhinos from unlawful hunting. These endeavors include expanded reconnaissance, local area commitment, and the

arrangement of hostile to poaching units to prevent and catch poachers. Examples of overcoming adversity in certain districts exhibit the adequacy of such drives in controling poaching.

2. **Local area Based Preservation:**
Connecting with neighborhood networks in rhino protection is vital to maintainable endeavors. Local area based preservation drives include training, elective work projects, and associations that engage neighborhood inhabitants to become stewards of their regular legacy. At the point when networks see unmistakable advantages from rhino preservation, they are bound to partake in security endeavors effectively.

3. **Movement and Renewed introduction Projects:**

Movement and renewed introduction programs mean to lay out or reinforce rhino populaces in reasonable living spaces. Rhinos are moved from regions with high populace densities to environments where they generally happened or where populaces need expansion. Fruitful renewed introduction programs add to the recuperation of rhino populaces and the rebuilding of biological capabilities.

VII. Future Points of view and Difficulties

1. **Adjusting Preservation and Advancement:**
Future preservation endeavors for rhinos should explore the fragile harmony between protecting biodiversity and advancing reasonable turn of events. Techniques that coordinate preservation with local area needs, land use arranging, and monetary advancement are fundamental for guaranteeing the drawn out concurrence of rhinos and human populaces.

2. **Worldwide Cooperation and Strategy Support:**
The preservation of rhinos requires worldwide cooperation and strategy support. Global endeavors to battle the unlawful untamed life exchange, reinforce natural life insurance regulations, and encourage participation between nations are pivotal for tending to the transboundary idea of rhino protection.

3. **Environmental Change Contemplations:**

Environmental change presents extra difficulties for rhino preservation. Modified atmospheric conditions, living space moves, and changes in vegetation sythesis may affect rhino territories. Understanding and relieving the impacts of environmental change on rhino biological systems will be vital for their drawn out endurance.

Chapter 1

The Keystone Role of Rhinos

Rhinos, magnificent and ancient animals, assume a vital part in keeping up with the sensitive equilibrium of environments across the globe. As cornerstone species, they apply a significant impact on their territories, forming the scene, advancing biodiversity, and adding to the general wellbeing of environments. This paper investigates the complex meaning of rhinos, analyzing their natural, social, and monetary significance, as well as the difficulties they face in the advanced world.

Environmental Importance

Rhinos, having a place with the family Rhinocerotidae, are herbivorous vertebrates that have meandered the Earth for a long period of time. Regardless of their impressive appearance, they are delicate goliaths with a basic environmental job. One of the critical commitments of rhinos to biological systems is their job in forming vegetation. As programs, rhinos feed on various plants, impacting the creation and construction of vegetation in their environments. This specific taking care of conduct keeps specific plant species from ruling the scene, advancing biodiversity by making a mosaic of various plant networks.

Also, rhinos are known as biological system engineers. Through their taking care of, floundering, and touching exercises, they alter their environmental factors, making microhabitats for different species. Rhinos' floundering conduct, where they roll in mud to chill off and safeguard their skin from parasites, makes despondencies in the ground that load up with water. These mud flounders become fundamental water hotspots for various different creatures, especially during dry seasons. This designing job makes rhinos instrumental in the endurance of different species in their biological systems.

Biodiversity Watchmen

Rhinos are overseers of biodiversity, impacting the overflow and dispersion of both widely varied vegetation in their territories. By keeping specific plant species from becoming predominant, rhinos permit a different cluster of plants to flourish. This, thus, upholds a great many herbivores and, consequently, hunters. The perplexing trap of collaborations made by rhinos adds to the flexibility of biological systems, making them more versatile to ecological changes.

Notwithstanding their effect on vegetation, rhinos are fundamental for keeping up with solid populaces of various different species. They make and keep up with open spaces through their taking care of, which benefits nibblers and different herbivores.

The presence of rhinos additionally impacts the way of behaving of hunters, as their excrement and fragrance markings can deflect or draw in specific hunters. This complicated exchange of natural connections highlights the cornerstone job of rhinos in saving biodiversity.

Social Importance

Past their environmental significance, rhinos hold tremendous social importance in different social orders. These radiant animals have been loved and represented in the fables, legends, and otherworldly convictions of many societies over the entire course of time. In a few African societies, the rhinoceros is related with strength, versatility, and security. The rhinoceros horn, in spite of being made out of keratin, similar substance as human hair and nails, has been generally esteemed in a few customary Asian societies for its apparent restorative properties and as a superficial point of interest.

The profound imagery of rhinos stretches out to their depiction in workmanship and writing. Old cavern canvases, ancestral workmanship, and contemporary works frequently portray rhinos as strong images of nature's greatness and the interconnectedness of every single living being. The social meaning of rhinos stresses the well established association between human social orders and the regular world, highlighting the significance of moderating these superb animals for people in the future.

Financial Significance and Ecotourism

Rhinos additionally contribute fundamentally to nearby economies through ecotourism. Nature stores and public stops that are home to rhino populaces draw in travelers from around the world. Natural life aficionados, photographic artists, and eco-voyagers run to these objections, producing income that upholds preservation endeavors and neighborhood networks. The monetary worth of rhinos reaches out past the travel industry, as their presence in safeguarded regions adds to the general strength of biological systems, guaranteeing the supportability of regular assets and advancing ecological solidness.

Moreover, the insurance and preservation of rhino populaces set out business open doors for nearby networks. Preservation drives require a gifted labor force for hostile to poaching watches, living space the board, and local area commitment. By putting resources into rhino protection, nations can animate monetary improvement while at the same time shielding biodiversity.

Challenges Confronting Rhinos

Notwithstanding their biological, social, and monetary significance, rhinos face various dangers that risk their endurance. Boss among these dangers is poaching, driven by the unlawful exchange rhino horns.

The interest for rhino horns, filled by misinformed convictions in their restorative properties and social importance, has prompted a staggering decrease in rhino populaces. Rhino poaching is a rewarding criminal venture, and coordinated wrongdoing networks frequently exploit devastated networks to complete these criminal operations.

Territory misfortune represents one more critical test for rhinos. As human populaces grow and infringe upon regular territories, the accessible space for rhinos lessens. Deforestation, agribusiness, and framework improvement further part rhino territories, making it challenging for populaces to flourish. Environmental change adds an extra layer of pressure, adjusting the accessibility of water and food assets and worsening existing dangers.

Protection Endeavors and Examples of overcoming adversity

Endeavors to save rhinos and address the difficulties they face have picked up speed as of late. Preservation associations, legislatures, and neighborhood networks are co-operating to execute techniques for safeguarding rhinos and their territories. Against poaching drives, utilizing trend setting innovation and thoroughly prepared work force, have been fruitful in controling unlawful hunting. Moreover, people group based preservation programs that include neighborhood occupants in rhino security have shown positive outcomes by making a feeling of shared liability and helping the two individuals and untamed life.

Movement projects, where rhinos are moved to more secure environments or once again introduced to regions where they were once extirpated, have likewise added to the recuperation of rhino populaces. These undertakings plan to lay out new populaces and guarantee hereditary variety, diminishing the gamble of inbreeding and improving the drawn out endurance possibilities of rhinos.

1.1 Rhinos as Keystone Species

Rhinos, with their monumental presence and old heredity, arise as quintessential cornerstone species, standing firm on a basic foothold in the mind boggling embroidery of Earth's biological systems. This article dives into the diverse job of rhinos as cornerstone species, explaining their biological importance, social significance, and the difficulties they face in the contemporary world. From molding scenes to epitomizing social imagery and adding to the economy through ecotourism, rhinos assume a significant part that reaches out a long ways past their actual presence.

1. **Natural Meaning of Rhinos**
1. **Territory Designing**

    Rhinos, individuals from the family Rhinocerotidae, have unmistakable biological qualities that make them irreplaceable in molding their environments. Their herbivorous nature positions them as crucial players in the guideline of vegetation. By specifically benefiting from various plant species, rhinos keep any one kind from overwhelming the scene, cultivating a different cluster of greenery. This specific perusing keeps up with biodiversity as well as guarantees the strength of biological systems to ecological vacillations.

2. **Biological system Designers**

The impact of rhinos stretches out past simple herbivory. Rhinos are viewed as environment engineers, effectively altering their environmental elements through different exercises like taking care of, floundering, and brushing. The floundering conduct, where rhinos roll in mud, not just guides in temperature guideline and parasite control yet in addition makes sorrows in the ground that act as fundamental water hotspots for various different species. This one of a kind mix of exercises changes the scene, making microhabitats that benefit an extensive variety of verdure.

3. **Roundabout Consequences for Fauna**

Rhinos, as herbivores, by implication influence different species by making and keeping up with open spaces through their taking care of exercises. This change of vegetation upholds slow eaters and different herbivores, framing a flowing impact that impacts the way of behaving and dissemination of hunters inside the biological system. Rhinos, subsequently, contribute fundamentally to the mind boggling trap of communications among various species, upgrading the general biodiversity and environmental equilibrium.

II. Rhinos as Biodiversity Watchmen

1. **Vegetation Elements**

The particular taking care of conduct of rhinos adds to the unique idea of vegetation in their territories. By forestalling the predominance of explicit plant species, rhinos make a mosaic of various plant networks. This, thusly, encourages a different cluster of herbivores and gives various assets to hunters. The complicated transaction between rhinos, vegetation, and other creature species features their job as biodiversity watchmen, guaranteeing the wellbeing and versatility of environments.

2. **Microhabitats and Species Associations**

Rhinos, through their exercises, for example, floundering and touching, make microhabitats that are significant for the endurance of different species.

The mud flounders, as well as filling in as water sources, become centers of movement for bugs, birds, and little warm blooded creatures. The fragrance markings and manure of rhinos impact the way of behaving of hunters, going about as signs that either draw in or discourage them. This perplexing organization of species connections highlights the cornerstone job of rhinos in forming and keeping up with the biodiversity of their environments.

III. Social Meaning of Rhinos

1. **Imagery and Folklore**
   Rhinos have held a critical spot in the fables, folklore, and social imagery of different social orders over the entire course of time. In a few African societies, rhinos are loved as images of solidarity, versatility, and security. The rhinoceros horn, however experimentally made out of keratin, has been generally esteemed in specific customary Asian societies for its apparent restorative properties and as a superficial point of interest. The otherworldly imagery of rhinos reaches out to their portrayal in workmanship, writing, and strict works on, stressing the significant association among people and the regular world.
2. **Protection Stories**

The social meaning of rhinos reaches out to contemporary preservation accounts. Rhinos, frequently depicted as leader species, become images of more extensive protection endeavors. The situation of rhinos because of poaching and territory misfortune has resounded with individuals universally, starting protection developments and drives. Social proclivity towards these lofty animals plays had a significant impact in earning public help for rhino protection, overcoming any issues between different societies and cultivating a common obligation regarding the prosperity of rhinos and their environments.

IV. Monetary Significance and Ecotourism

1. **Monetary Commitments**
   Rhinos, as cornerstone species, contribute fundamentally to neighborhood economies through ecotourism. Safeguarded regions and public stops that harbor rhino populaces become magnets for travelers, producing income that upholds both protection endeavors and neighborhood networks. Untamed life fans, photographic artists, and ecotourists add to the economy while encountering the marvel of rhinos in their regular living spaces. Past the travel industry, the preservation of rhinos sets out work open doors for neighborhood networks, going from against poaching watches to territory the board.
2. **Manageable Turn of events**

Interest in rhino preservation lines up with standards of practical turn of events. By saving rhino populaces, nations can guarantee the supported accessibility of normal assets, keep up with the natural equilibrium, and advance ecological strength. This double advantage - financial increase and natural supportability - positions rhino protection as a model for mindful and feasible turn of events, exhibiting the potential for fitting human exercises with the conservation of cornerstone species and their environments.

V. Challenges Confronting Rhinos

1. **Poaching and Unlawful Exchange**
   Notwithstanding their natural, social, and financial significance, rhinos face imposing difficulties that undermine their reality. Boss among these is the tireless danger of poaching driven by the unlawful exchange rhino horns. Rhino horns, dishonestly accepted to have restorative properties and social importance, bring excessive costs on the bootleg market. The interest for rhino horns energizes a worthwhile unlawful exchange, prompting a staggering decrease in rhino populaces and representing a serious danger to their endurance.

2. **Environment Misfortune and Discontinuity**
   Environment misfortune, driven by human exercises like agribusiness, foundation advancement, and deforestation, presents one more critical test for rhinos. As human populaces grow, normal environments psychologist, and rhinos are constrained into more modest and more divided regions. This territory misfortune restricts the accessible space for rhinos as well as upsets their capacity to move and connect inside their environments. The fracture of living spaces expands the weakness of rhino populaces, making them more vulnerable to outside dangers.

3. **Environmental Change**

The general test of environmental change further mixtures the dangers looked by rhinos. Changes in temperature, precipitation designs, and the recurrence of outrageous climate occasions can modify the accessibility of water and food assets. These changes in ecological circumstances influence rhinos as well as the whole biological system, influencing the conveyance and wealth of plant and creature species. Environmental change fuels existing dangers, making a perplexing and interconnected trap of difficulties for rhino protection.

VI. Protection Endeavors and Examples of overcoming adversity

1. **Hostile to Poaching Drives**
   Protection associations, legislatures, and nearby networks have assembled to address the difficulties confronting rhinos. Hostile to poaching drives, outfitted with trend setting innovation and thoroughly prepared staff, have shown progress in controling unlawful hunting. The utilization of robots, satellite following, and refined observing frameworks has upgraded the adequacy of against poaching endeavors, stopping poachers and defending rhino populaces.

2. **Local area Based Preservation**
   Local area based preservation programs have arisen as a fruitful technique for rhino security. Connecting with nearby networks in protection endeavors makes a feeling of shared liability and engages occupants to become stewards of their normal legacy. By affecting nearby individuals in enemy of poaching watches, natural surroundings rebuilding, and schooling drives, preservation associations

encourage a practical way to deal with rhino security that benefits the two individuals and untamed life.

3. **Movement and Renewed introduction**

   Movement projects, including the development of rhinos to more secure environments or their renewed introduction to regions where they were once extirpated, play had a pivotal impact in rhino protection. These tasks intend to lay out new populaces, guarantee hereditary variety, and decrease the gamble of inbreeding. Fruitful movements add to the recuperation of rhino populaces and exhibit the potential for human mediation to relieve the effects of territory misfortune and poaching.

4. **Global Coordinated effort**

Rhino protection has turned into a worldwide undertaking, with nations, associations, and people teaming up to address the transboundary idea of the difficulties looked by rhinos. Peaceful accords, for example, the Show on Worldwide Exchange Imperiled Types of Wild Fauna and Vegetation (Refers to), assume a urgent part in directing the exchange of rhino items and planning protection endeavors on a worldwide scale. The trading of information, assets, and mastery encourages an aggregate way to deal with safeguarding rhinos and their biological systems.

1.2 Historical Significance of Rhinos in Ecosystems

Rhinos, with their ancient heredity and imposing presence, have carved a significant history in the records of Earth's biological systems. This exposition sets out on an ordered investigation of the verifiable meaning of rhinos, following their development through time and the essential job they have played in forming scenes, cultivating biodiversity, and making a permanent imprint on the regular world.

1. **Rhinos Through Topographical Ages**
1. **Antiquated Beginnings**

   The authentic excursion of rhinos follows back great many years, with proof proposing their presence during the Oligocene age. Fossil records uncover the assorted developmental ways rhinos have taken, adjusting to different ecological circumstances and advancing into various species. The rise of rhinos is a demonstration of their strength and flexibility, exhibiting their capacity to explore the changing scenes of Earth's set of experiences.

2. **Developmental Variety**

As the land ages unfurled, rhinos expanded into various species, each adjusted to explicit natural specialties. The wooly rhinoceros, for example, flourished in the virus environments of the Pleistocene age, while different species adjusted to tropical and subtropical conditions. This transformative variety features the job of rhinos as natural trailblazers, molding their qualities because of the powerful states of Earth's set of experiences.

II. Rhinos as Megafauna

1. Pleistocene Megafauna

During the Pleistocene age, rhinos were important for a different cluster of megafauna that wandered the Earth. Huge herbivores, including mammoths, monster sloths, and different rhino species, assumed a vital part in forming scenes through their taking care of propensities and connections with vegetation. The verifiable meaning of rhinos during this period lies in their commitment to the mosaic of biological systems, impacting the appropriation and wealth of plant species.

2. Coevolution with Plants

Rhinos, as herbivores, participated in many-sided associations with the vegetation of their natural surroundings. The particular taking care of conduct of rhinos affected the piece of vegetation, forestalling the predominance of specific plant species and cultivating biodiversity. This coevolutionary dance among rhinos and plants highlighted their authentic job as natural powerhouses, adding to the unique harmony of Pleistocene environments.

III. Connections with Early People

1. Paleolithic Workmanship and Imagery

The verifiable association among rhinos and people traces all the way back to the Paleolithic time. Cave artistic creations found in different regions of the planet portray rhinos close by other megafauna, offering looks into the existences of early people.

These imaginative portrayals recommend that rhinos held social importance for early human social orders, potentially representing strength, flexibility, or a profound association with the regular world.

2. Use of Rhino Assets

Past imagery, early people probably interfaced with rhinos as a wellspring of assets. Rhinoceros bones and stows away might have been utilized for apparatuses, sanctuary, or dress. The verifiable entwining of rhinos and human endurance features their concurrence and the biological reliance between species, even in the beginning phases of mankind's set of experiences.

IV. Social Importance in Old Social orders

1. Rhinos in Folklore and Religion

Rhinos have held social importance in different old social orders, becoming images in legends, old stories, and strict convictions. In a few African societies, rhinos were respected as strong creatures related with security and shrewdness. The rhinoceros horn, in spite of being made out of keratin, turned into a sought after object with apparent supernatural properties, prompting its fuse in customary ceremonies and practices.

2. **Authentic Stories**

The authentic meaning of rhinos rises above their biological job and crosses with the stories of antiquated human advancements. The excursions of pioneers, dealers, and explorers frequently entwined with experiences with rhinos, molding authentic records and impression of these superb animals. Rhinos, as magnetic megafauna, left an engraving on the authentic awareness of social orders across the globe.

V. Pioneer Period and Double-dealing

1. **Chasing after Prizes and Examples**
   The frontier time got a shift the connection among people and rhinos. European wayfarers and pilgrims saw rhinos as extraordinary prizes and looked to gather examples for logical review. This period denoted the start of double-dealing and the commodification of rhinos, as their horns and stows away became sought-after things in the thriving exchange organizations of the time.

2. **Decrease in Populace**

The verifiable double-dealing of rhinos, driven by provincial interests, added to a huge decrease in their populaces. Chasing after prizes, living space obliteration, and the rising infringement of human exercises prompted a decrease in rhino numbers.

The repercussions of this authentic double-dealing resonate through time, affecting the preservation challenges looked by rhinos in the cutting edge period.

VI. Preservation Arousing and the twentieth Hundred years

1. **Early Preservation Endeavors**
   The twentieth century saw a developing consciousness of the predicament of rhinos and other imperiled species. Progressives, researchers, and concerned people started to perceive the authentic effect of human exercises on rhino populaces. Early preservation endeavors zeroed in on laying out safeguarded regions and bringing issues to light about the environmental significance of rhinos trying to turn around the authentic pattern of populace decline.

2. **Rhinos as Lead Species**

Rhinos arose as lead species for protection, representing the more extensive difficulties looked by biodiversity. Preservation associations utilized the magnetic allure of rhinos to gather public help, starting a worldwide development to safeguard these famous animals. The verifiable meaning of rhinos turned into a mobilizing point for the more extensive protection plan, underscoring the need to safeguard biodiversity and the wellbeing of environments.

VII. Current Difficulties and Protection Methodologies

1. **Poaching Pestilence**

   Regardless of authentic protection endeavors, rhinos face exceptional difficulties in the cutting edge time. The resurgence of poaching, driven by the unlawful exchange rhino horns, represents a serious danger to their endurance. The verifiable double-dealing of rhinos for prizes and assets has developed into a modern and worthwhile criminal venture, filling the interest for their horns in a few customary Asian business sectors.

2. **Environment Misfortune and Discontinuity**

   The authentic story of natural surroundings misfortune keeps on unfurling in the advanced period. As human populaces extend, regular natural surroundings shrivel, prompting expanded fracture and corruption of rhino living spaces. Urbanization, horticulture, and framework improvement further worsen the difficulties looked by rhinos, restricting their accessible space and disturbing critical biological cycles.

3. **Environmental Change**

   In the 21st 100 years, the authentic difficulties looked by rhinos are intensified by the general danger of environmental change. Changes in temperature, precipitation designs, and the recurrence of outrageous climate occasions influence the accessibility of water and food assets, impacting the conveyance and conduct of the two rhinos and the species with which they cooperate. Environmental change adds a layer of intricacy to the verifiable difficulties looked by rhinos and requires versatile preservation methodologies.

4. **Preservation Developments**

In light of the contemporary difficulties, preservationists are utilizing imaginative procedures established in authentic illustrations. Cutting edge innovations, like satellite following, drones, and hereditary checking, upgrade against poaching endeavors and add to the logical comprehension of rhino biology. Local area based preservation drives, propelled by authentic concurrence among people and rhinos, draw in neighborhood networks as partners in the security of these magnificent animals.

VIII. The Continuous Tradition of Rhinos

1. **Protection Examples of overcoming adversity**

   In the midst of the difficulties, there are examples of overcoming adversity that highlight the strength of rhinos and the adequacy of protection endeavors.

Movement projects, natural surroundings reclamation drives, and local area association have added to the recuperation of rhino populaces in specific districts. These examples of overcoming adversity act as encouraging signs, showing the way that verifiable patterns can be turned around through committed preservation activities.

2. **Instructive Drives**

The verifiable meaning of rhinos is progressively turning into a point of convergence of instructive drives. Natural training programs, outreach missions, and narratives feature the significance of rhinos with regards to Earth's set of experiences. By encouraging a comprehension of the verifiable exchange among rhinos and environments, these drives plan to motivate people in the future to take part in protection and economical practices effectively.

1.3Current Status of Rhino Populations

The ongoing status of rhino populaces remains at a basic crossroads, molded by an intricate interchange of biological, social, and financial variables. As charming megafauna and cornerstone species, rhinos assume a urgent part in keeping up with environment balance.

This paper gives an inside and out investigation of the ongoing circumstance, inspecting the difficulties confronting rhino populaces, progressing preservation endeavors, and the cooperative drives pointed toward getting a future for these glorious animals.

1. **Outline of Rhino Species**

1. **Species Variety**

Rhinos are addressed by five surviving species, each with extraordinary attributes and environment inclinations. These species incorporate the White Rhino (Ceratotherium simum), Dark Rhino (Diceros bicornis), Indian Rhino (Rhinoceros unicornis), Javan Rhino (Rhinoceros sondaicus), and Sumatran Rhino (Dicerorhinus sumatrensis). The dispersion of these species traverses Africa and Asia, with fluctuating levels of danger.

2. **Conveyance and Risk**

The conveyance of rhino species is lopsided, with African rhinos essentially occupying savannas and prairies, while Asian rhinos are tracked down in tropical and subtropical woodlands. The Dark Rhino and the Javan Rhino are basically imperiled, confronting extreme populace declines, while the White Rhino, Indian Rhino, and Sumatran Rhino are likewise delegated defenseless or jeopardized. The assorted status of rhino species mirrors the limited and worldwide dangers they face.

II. Key Dangers to Rhino Populaces

1. **Poaching for Rhino Horns**

   The most prompt and extreme danger to rhino populaces is poaching driven by the unlawful exchange rhino horns. Rhino horns are erroneously accepted to have therapeutic properties in a few conventional Asian societies, filling an interest that drives poaching to disturbing levels. Criminal organizations, frequently efficient and vigorously equipped, exploit this interest, prompting the terrible loss of rhinos and compromising the endurance of whole populaces.

2. **Natural surroundings Misfortune and Discontinuity**

   The verifiable pattern of natural surroundings misfortune and discontinuity keeps on tormenting rhino populaces. As human populaces grow, normal living spaces are infringed upon for horticulture, urbanization, and foundation improvement. This diminishes the accessible space for rhinos as well as disturbs basic natural cycles, making it provoking for populaces to flourish and lessening their general flexibility to ecological changes.

3. **Environmental Change**

   The general danger of environmental change adds a layer of intricacy to the difficulties looked by rhinos. Modifications in temperature, precipitation designs, and the recurrence of outrageous climate occasions can affect the dispersion and overflow of vegetation, water assets, and the accessibility of reasonable natural surroundings. Rhinos, previously wrestling with poaching and living space misfortune, should now fight with the more extensive outcomes of an evolving environment.

4. **Human-Untamed life Struggle**

As human populaces venture into rhino territories, clashes among people and rhinos heighten. Crop harm, wounds, and fatalities result from cooperations among rhinos and neighborhood networks. These struggles further strain rhino populaces, compounding the difficulties they face and adding to negative view of rhinos among impacted networks.

III. Preservation Drives and Methodologies

1. **Against Poaching Measures**

   Because of the flood in poaching, preservation associations and legislatures have executed thorough enemy of poaching measures. These drives incorporate the organization of cutting edge innovations like robots, satellite following, and infrared cameras to screen rhino populaces. Thoroughly prepared enemy of poaching units watch safeguarded regions, intending to block and deflect poachers before they can cause hurt for rhinos.

2. **Local area Based Preservation**

   Perceiving the significance of connecting with nearby networks, numerous preservation drives have taken on local area based approaches. These projects include nearby occupants in preservation endeavors, giving monetary motivators and cultivating a feeling of shared liability. By adjusting protection objectives to local area interests, these drives try to make an amicable concurrence among people and rhinos.

3. **Movement and Renewed introduction**

   Movement projects, including the development of rhinos to more secure natural surroundings or their renewed introduction to regions where they were once extirpated, have become indispensable to protection techniques. These activities plan to lay out new populaces, improve hereditary variety, and lessen the gamble of inbreeding. Fruitful movements add to the recuperation of rhino populaces and assist with getting their drawn out endurance.

4. **Global Cooperation**

   The worldwide idea of the difficulties confronting rhinos requires global joint effort. Associations, for example, the Show on Global Exchange Imperiled Types of Wild Fauna and Greenery (Refers to) assume a urgent part in managing the exchange of rhino items and organizing preservation endeavors. Cooperative drives include numerous nations, NGOs, and partners cooperating to address the transboundary idea of the dangers looked by rhinos.

5. **Official Measures**

Numerous nations have executed severe regulative measures to battle poaching and unlawful exchange. Punishments for rhino-related wrongdoings have been expanded, and policing team up with protection associations to arraign people associated with criminal operations. Reinforcing lawful systems and requirement components is basic to checking the interest for rhino horns and disturbing unlawful exchange organizations.

IV. Examples of overcoming adversity and Positive Patterns

Regardless of the horde challenges, there are cases of progress and positive patterns in rhino protection. A populaces have balanced out or expanded because of purposeful endeavors, showing that with compelling protection techniques, switching the decay of rhino populations is conceivable. Preservation examples of overcoming adversity give motivation and bits of knowledge into the variables that add to positive results.

1. **Populace Expansions in Specific Stores**

   In unambiguous saves and safeguarded regions, rhino populaces have given indications of recuperation. Hearty enemy of poaching measures, local area commitment, and natural surroundings rebuilding endeavors have added to the outcome of these drives. Outstanding models incorporate the populace increments of white rhinos in specific South African stores, displaying the potential for protection mediations to yield positive outcomes.

2. **Local area Backing and Mindfulness**

The contribution of nearby networks in preservation drives has been instrumental in accomplishing positive results. Building mindfulness about the biological significance of rhinos and accumulating nearby help adds to the progress of hostile to poaching endeavors and living space preservation. Local area individuals become advocates for rhino insurance, making an organization of help that upgrades the viability of preservation measures.

V. Continuous Difficulties and Arising Issues

1. **Tireless Dangers**
   Notwithstanding the headway verified regions, rhino populaces keep on confronting constant and advancing dangers. The interest for rhino horns stays high, determined by well established social convictions and the productivity of the unlawful exchange. However long this request perseveres, rhinos will be powerless against poaching, requiring supported endeavors to battle the unlawful natural life exchange.

2. **Versatile Procedures for Environmental Change**
   The ramifications of environmental change represent a continuous test for rhino preservation. Progressives should foster versatile methodologies to assist rhino populaces with adapting to the changing natural circumstances. This might include territory rebuilding, the formation of environment strong hallways, and checking the effects of environmental change on rhino conduct and wellbeing.

3. **Adjusting Protection and Advancement**

As human populaces keep on developing, finding a harmony among protection and improvement turns out to be progressively complicated. Preservation endeavors should explore the contending requests for land, assets, and financial turn of events. Manageable improvement rehearses that consider the necessities of the two people and rhinos are fundamental for accomplishing long haul conjunction.

VI. The Job of Innovation in Preservation

Progressions in innovation have become important apparatuses in the preservation weapons store. From satellite following and robots for checking rhino developments to hereditary observing for evaluating populace wellbeing, innovation assumes a urgent part in upgrading the productivity and viability of preservation endeavors. The reconciliation of state of the art advancements adds to the improvement of imaginative techniques for rhino insurance.

VII. Future Possibilities and the Street Ahead

1. **Long haul Preservation Objectives**
   What's in store possibilities of rhino populaces rely on the aggregate responsibility of states, preservation associations, nearby networks, and the worldwide

local area. Long haul protection objectives incorporate accomplishing reasonable populaces, saving hereditary variety, and getting natural surroundings that permit rhinos to flourish. Tending to the main drivers of dangers, like interest decrease for rhino items, is significant for supported achievement.

2. **Worldwide Support and Instruction**

   Worldwide support and instruction drives are fundamental parts of getting a future for rhinos. Bringing issues to light about the biological significance of rhinos, the dangers they face, and the job people can play in preservation endeavors is foremost. By encouraging a worldwide comprehension of the difficulties and potential open doors, promotion drives add to the making of a strong organization for rhino preservation.

3. **Imaginative Protection Funding**

   Investigating imaginative protection supporting components is urgent for guaranteeing the supported financing of preservation drives. This might include associations with private area elements, generous associations, and the advancement of maintainable ecotourism models. Broadening subsidizing sources upgrades the monetary strength of preservation programs, taking into consideration proceeded with endeavors to safeguard rhinos.

4. **Versatile Administration**

Given the unique idea of environmental frameworks and the advancing difficulties looked by rhinos, versatile administration systems are fundamental. Protection programs should be adaptable, ready to answer evolving conditions, and integrate illustrations gained from the two triumphs and disappointments. Ordinary appraisals and changes guarantee that protection endeavors stay powerful and important after some time.

Chapter 2

Rhino Behavior and Habitat

Rhinos, glorious animals with a heredity extending back huge number of years, display a different cluster of ways of behaving complicatedly woven into the texture of their environments. This paper dives into the nuanced universe of rhino conduct and territory, investigating the biological meaning of their activities, the transformations that empower their endurance, and the protection challenges they face in the advanced time.

1. **Outline of Rhino Species and Dispersion**
1. **Rhino Species Variety**

   Rhinos, having a place with the family Rhinocerotidae, are addressed by five surviving species: the White Rhino (Ceratotherium simum), Dark Rhino (Diceros bicornis), Indian Rhino (Rhinoceros unicornis), Javan Rhino (Rhinoceros sondaicus), and Sumatran Rhino (Dicerorhinus sumatrensis). Every species has one of a kind qualities, ways of behaving, and transformations, adding to the rich biodiversity of the environments they occupy.

2. **Topographical Conveyance**

Rhinos are circulated across Africa and Asia, possessing various environments going from savannas and prairies to tropical and subtropical woods. The White Rhino, for instance, flourishes in verdant scenes, while the Dark Rhino adjusts to a more fluctuated living space, including savannas and thick shrublands. Understanding the geological appropriation of rhino species is basic to appreciating their way of behaving and biological jobs.

II. Rhino Conduct: Social Elements and Correspondence

1. **Social Design**

   Rhinos display different social designs, fluctuating among species and even inside populaces. The White Rhino is known for its generally friendly nature, frequently framing free gatherings called crashes. Interestingly, the Dark Rhino will in general be more lone, with people keeping up with bigger individual regions. Indian Rhinos, contingent upon the accessibility of assets, may show both singular and social ways of behaving.

2. **Correspondence and Vocalizations**

Correspondence is a critical part of rhino conduct, working with communications inside gatherings and flagging regional limits. Rhinos convey through different means, including vocalizations, non-verbal communication, and fragrance stamping.

While they are not known for being profoundly vocal, rhinos produce a scope of sounds, from snorts and thunders to trumpeting. Fragrance checking, accomplished through pee showering and compost heaps, assumes a huge part in passing on data about individual personality and regenerative status.

III. Taking care of Conduct and Dietary Inclinations

1. **Herbivorous Eating routine**

   Rhinos are fundamentally herbivores, and their taking care of conduct assumes an essential part in molding the environments they occupy. Their eating regimens comprise of an assortment of plant animal types, including grasses, bushes, and trees. The particular taking care of conduct of rhinos adds to vegetation control, forestalling the strength of explicit plants and encouraging biodiversity inside their territories.

2. **Special Mouth Construction**

Rhinos have special mouth structures adjusted to their herbivorous weight control plans. The White Rhino, portrayed by its wide mouth, is a nibbler that feeds on grasses. Interestingly, the Dark Rhino, with its snared upper lip, is a program that consumes leaves and branches from brambles and trees. The specific transformations of their mouths mirror the coevolutionary connection among rhinos and the vegetation in their natural surroundings.

IV. Conceptive Way of behaving and Parental Consideration

1. **Mating Customs**

   Regenerative conduct shifts among rhino species, with particular mating customs and romance presentations. Mating connections might include vocalizations, checking of regions, and actual showcases of predominance. The timing and recurrence of mating occasions are affected by variables like asset accessibility and ecological circumstances. Understanding the complexities of rhino conceptive way of behaving is fundamental for preservation endeavors pointed toward guaranteeing the drawn out reasonability of populaces.

2. **Growth and Birth**

Rhinos have moderately lengthy incubation periods, going from 15 to year and a half, contingent upon the species. Female rhinos ordinarily bring forth a solitary calf, and the mother gives care and insurance during the beginning phases of the calf's life. The improvement of a solid maternal bond is basic for the endurance of the calf, as rhino populaces face difficulties like predation and, all the more essentially, human-initiated dangers.

V. Natural surroundings Inclinations and Biological system Designing

1. **Fields, Savannas, and Woodlands**
   Rhinos possess an assorted scope of natural surroundings, exhibiting their versatility to various ecological circumstances. The White Rhino, for example, is appropriate to open meadows and savannas, where it can eat on bountiful grass species. Dark Rhinos, with their perusing conduct, can be tracked down in various territories, including savannas and thick shrublands. The Indian Rhino is adjusted to the muggy fields and backwoods of South Asia, while the Javan and Sumatran Rhinos are related with thick tropical and subtropical timberlands.

2. **Biological system Designing**

Rhinos are perceived as cornerstone species and biological system engineers because of their significant impact on their living spaces. Through their taking care of, floundering, and brushing ways of behaving, rhinos effectively shape the scenes they possess. The specific benefiting from vegetation forestalls the strength of specific plant species, cultivating biodiversity. Floundering makes mud discouragements that act as fundamental water hotspots for various species, while the aroma stamping of domains impacts the way of behaving of different creatures inside the biological system.

VI. Preservation Difficulties: Poaching and Territory Misfortune

1. **Poaching for Rhino Horns**
   The most squeezing danger to rhino populaces is poaching driven by the unlawful exchange rhino horns. Rhino horns, made out of keratin, have been mistakenly credited with therapeutic properties and social importance in specific customary Asian business sectors. This request fills a worthwhile bootleg market, prompting an overwhelming loss of rhinos across Africa and Asia. Hostile to poaching endeavors are significant in addressing this prompt danger to rhino endurance.

2. **Natural surroundings Misfortune and Discontinuity**

Environment misfortune and fracture present critical difficulties to rhino populaces. Human exercises, including agribusiness, urbanization, and framework advancement, infringe upon normal environments, diminishing the accessible space for rhinos. Fracture upsets the network between living spaces, restricting the development of rhino populaces and undermining their capacity to track down assets, mates, and reasonable favorable places.

VII. Preservation Procedures and Examples of overcoming adversity

1. **Against Poaching Drives**

   Protection associations and legislatures convey against poaching drives to battle the wild unlawful exchange rhino horns. These endeavors include exceptional and prepared enemy of poaching units, innovation like robots and satellite following, and global coordinated effort to destroy the crook networks behind the unlawful exchange. Progress in enemy of poaching measures is essential for the quick endurance of rhino populaces.

2. **Environment Assurance and Rebuilding**

   Saving and reestablishing rhino natural surroundings are central parts of protection methodologies. Safeguarded regions and public parks assume a critical part in giving places of refuge to rhinos, permitting populaces to recuperate and flourish. Environment rebuilding drives mean to address the effects of natural surroundings misfortune by restoring network between divided regions and advancing the recovery of key plant species.

3. **Local area Based Preservation**

   Connecting with nearby networks in preservation endeavors is basic to the outcome of rhino assurance. Local area based protection programs include occupants in enemy of poaching watches, living space reclamation, and schooling drives. By adjusting protection objectives to neighborhood interests and giving financial motivators, these projects encourage a feeling of shared liability and engage networks to become stewards of their regular legacy.

4. **Movement and Renewed introduction**

   Movement projects, including the development of rhinos to more secure natural surroundings or their renewed introduction to regions where they were once extirpated, add to the recuperation of rhino populaces. These drives expect to lay out new populaces, upgrade hereditary variety, and lessen the gamble of inbreeding. Fruitful movements feature the potential for human mediation to moderate the effects of verifiable difficulties looked by rhinos.

VIII. The Job of Exploration and Innovation

1. **Logical Exploration**

   Logical examination assumes an essential part in figuring out rhino conduct, nature, and populace elements. Scientists use strategies like satellite following, hereditary investigation, and natural demonstrating to acquire experiences into rhino developments, environment inclinations, and the elements affecting their endurance. This information frames the establishment for proof based protection techniques and versatile administration draws near.

2. **Innovation for Preservation**

Progressions in innovation have reformed preservation endeavors pointed toward safeguarding rhinos. Satellite following permits continuous observing of rhino developments, assisting against poaching units with answering quickly to dangers. Drones give airborne observation of immense scenes, upgrading the effectiveness of watches. Hereditary observing helps with surveying populace wellbeing and hereditary variety. The reconciliation of innovation into preservation rehearses enhances the effect of drives pointed toward defending rhinos.

IX. Arising Protection Difficulties and Future Bearings

1. **Environmental Change Effects**
   The apparition of environmental change presents new difficulties for rhino preservation. Changes in temperature, precipitation designs, and the recurrence of outrageous climate occasions can affect the accessibility of water and food assets, modifying the conveyance and conduct of rhinos. Preservation systems should adjust to the changing ecological circumstances, consolidating environment strong methodologies.

2. **Reasonable Turn of events and Human-Natural life Concurrence**
   Adjusting the necessities of human populaces with rhino protection is a continuous test. Reasonable advancement rehearses that consider the prosperity of the two people and rhinos are fundamental for accomplishing long haul concurrence. Drives that advance elective vocations, local area based ecotourism, and natural surroundings reclamation add to the agreeable coordination of human exercises and untamed life preservation.

3. **Worldwide Cooperation and Backing**
   The protection of rhinos requires a worldwide responsibility and cooperative endeavors. Global joint effort through associations like Refers to, alongside backing drives, is fundamental for tending to the transboundary idea of the difficulties looked by rhinos. Bringing issues to light about the natural significance of rhinos and the dangers they face encourages a feeling of divided liability between the worldwide local area.

4. **Instructive Drives**

Instructive projects assume a critical part in forming perspectives and cultivating a more profound comprehension of the environmental meaning of rhinos. Schools, colleges, and effort programs add to building a preservation disapproved of age that values biodiversity and effectively partakes in the security of rhinos and their living spaces. Instruction drives structure a basic mainstay of long haul preservation techniques.

2.1Rhino Species and Their Characteristics

Rhinos, old goliaths with a genealogy extending back large number of years, incorporate a different gathering of animal groups showing extraordinary qualities and variations. The five surviving rhino species — White Rhino, Dark Rhino, Indian Rhino, Javan Rhino, and Sumatran Rhino — possess particular living spaces across Africa and Asia. This article dives into the singular attributes of every species, investigating their actual characteristics, ways of behaving, and natural jobs, while additionally tending to the difficulties they experience in the cutting edge world.

1. **White Rhino (Ceratotherium simum)**
   Actual Qualities

   The White Rhino remains as the biggest rhino species, portrayed by its strong form and an articulated protuberance on the rear of its neck. Grown-up guys of this species can arrive at stunning loads of as much as 2,300 kilograms, solidly laying out them as one of the heaviest land vertebrates. A remarkable element recognizing the White Rhino is its wide, square-molded mouth, explicitly adjusted for munching on grasses. This mouth structure diverges from the more prehensile lips found in other rhino species, which are outfitted towards perusing on leaves and twigs.

   Conduct and Social Design

   White Rhinos display a generally friendly nature, frequently shaping free gatherings known as accidents. These accidents ordinarily incorporate females, calves, and adolescents, with prevailing guys declaring their presence inside the gathering. The social elements inside an accident include correspondence through different means. While White Rhinos are not profoundly vocal, they utilize non-verbal communication, vocalizations, and aroma stamping to pass on data about character, regenerative status, and domain.

2. **Dark Rhino (Diceros bicornis)**
   Actual Attributes

   Rather than the White Rhino, the Dark Rhino has a more slim and nimble form. Grown-up Dark Rhinos weigh extensively not exactly their White Rhino partners, with guys averaging around 800 to 1,400 kilograms. One unmistakable actual component of the Dark Rhino is its snared upper lip, adjusted for getting a handle on leaves and twigs from brambles and trees during perusing.

   Conduct and Social Design

   Dark Rhinos are known for their transcendently lone way of behaving. Dissimilar to the more friendly White Rhino, Dark Rhinos lay out bigger individual domains, mirroring their inclination for a more single way of life.

   This singular way of behaving reaches out to their taking care of propensities, where they peruse on a different exhibit of vegetation. While less vocal than White Rhinos, Dark Rhinos impart through non-verbal communication, intermittent vocalizations, and aroma checking to depict their regions and pass on conceptive data.

3. **Indian Rhino (Rhinoceros unicornis)**
Actual Qualities

The Indian Rhino, otherwise called the More noteworthy One-Horned Rhino, flaunts unmistakable actual attributes that put it aside from its African partners. Grown-up guys weigh somewhere in the range of 2,000 and 2,300 kilograms, looking like the White Rhino regarding size. Outstandingly, the Indian Rhino includes a solitary horn, rather than the two horns present in African rhino species. Their skin is portrayed by noticeable folds, giving them an exceptional appearance.

Conduct and Social Design

Indian Rhinos are semi-oceanic and all around adjusted to marshy fields and backwoods. They display both single and social ways of behaving, affected by the accessibility of assets. During the dry season, Indian Rhinos are bound to take on a single way of life, while the wet season empowers social collaborations. Correspondence includes vocalizations, non-verbal communication, and fragrance stamping, with females especially vocal during the mating season.

4. **Javan Rhino (Rhinoceros sondaicus)**
Actual Attributes

The Javan Rhino, one of the most uncommon and most imperiled rhino species, shows interesting actual elements. Grown-up Javan Rhinos are more modest in size contrasted with their African partners, with guys gauging around 900 to 1,400 kilograms. They have a solitary horn, similar as the Indian Rhino, and have a generally little and minimal form. Their skin misses the mark on conspicuous folds found in Indian Rhinos.

Conduct and Social Design

Javan Rhinos are known for their slippery and lone nature. They basically possess thick tropical and subtropical backwoods, mentioning direct objective facts testing. Restricted data on their way of behaving recommends that they impart through vocalizations and aroma checking. The shortage of the Javan Rhino highlights the basic protection challenges looked by this species.

5. **Sumatran Rhino (Dicerorhinus sumatrensis)**

Actual Attributes

The Sumatran Rhino, the littlest of the living rhino species, displays particular actual qualities. Grown-up guys weigh somewhere in the range of 700 and 950 kilograms. Not at all like other rhino species, Sumatran Rhinos have hair, giving them a shaggy appearance. They likewise have two horns, with the back horn commonly longer than the foremost one.

Conduct and Social Construction

Sumatran Rhinos are known for their singular way of behaving, and they basically possess thick tropical and subtropical woods. Their single nature reaches out to their taking care of propensities, where they scrounge for an assortment of vegetation. Restricted data on Sumatran Rhino conduct shows that they use vocalizations, including whistles and different sounds, for correspondence. The slippery idea of this species adds to the difficulties of examining and rationing them.

Preservation Difficulties and Techniques

All rhino species face huge preservation challenges, fundamentally determined by poaching for their horns and living space misfortune. The interest for rhino horns, powered by social convictions and the unlawful natural life exchange, represents a quick danger to their endurance. Preservation procedures incorporate enemy of poaching measures, living space assurance and rebuilding, local area based protection drives, and worldwide coordinated efforts.

Against Poaching Measures

Endeavors to battle poaching include the sending of exceptional and prepared enemy of poaching units, innovation like robots and satellite following, and worldwide cooperation to destroy the lawbreaker networks behind the unlawful exchange. The outcome of these drives is urgent for the prompt endurance of rhino populaces.

Natural surroundings Insurance and Reclamation

Protecting and reestablishing rhino environments are crucial parts of preservation techniques. Safeguarded regions and public parks assume a vital part in giving places of refuge to rhinos, permitting populaces to recuperate and flourish. Territory reclamation drives expect to address the effects of natural surroundings misfortune by restoring availability between divided regions and advancing the recovery of key plant species.

Local area Based Protection

Drawing in nearby networks in preservation endeavors is basic to the progress of rhino security. Local area based protection programs include occupants in enemy of poaching watches, environment reclamation, and training drives. By adjusting preservation objectives to nearby interests and giving financial motivating forces, these projects encourage a feeling of shared liability and engage networks to become stewards of their normal legacy.

Movement and Renewed introduction

Movement projects, including the development of rhinos to more secure environments or their renewed introduction to regions where they were once extirpated, add to the recuperation of rhino populaces. These drives expect to lay out new populaces, improve hereditary variety, and lessen the gamble of inbreeding. Effective movements grandstand the potential for human intercession to moderate the effects of authentic difficulties looked by rhinos.

2.2 Rhino Habitat Requirements

The environment prerequisites of rhinos assume a critical part in their endurance and prosperity. Understanding the particular necessities of various rhino species is essential for compelling preservation methodologies. This exposition investigates the different living space necessities of rhinos, taking into account the particular inclinations and variations of species like the White Rhino, Dark Rhino, Indian Rhino, Javan Rhino, and Sumatran Rhino. By digging into the complexities of their territories, we gain experiences into the difficulties they face and the fundamental measures expected to guarantee their proceeded with presence.

1. **White Rhino Territory Necessities**

   The White Rhino, described by its wide mouth adjusted for nibbling on grasses, flourishes in open fields and savannas. These far reaching scenes give the best climate to their brushing conduct. Water sources are urgent for White Rhinos, and their living spaces frequently incorporate water openings or streams where they can drink and flounder. The transparency of the natural surroundings takes into consideration social associations inside crashes, where people impart and lay out strength.

   Protection endeavors for White Rhinos center around safeguarding these huge field environments, guaranteeing admittance to water sources, and relieving dangers like poaching and territory infringement. Safeguarded regions and public parks assume a basic part in giving places of refuge to White Rhinos, permitting them to keep up with their trademark social designs and conduct.

2. **Dark Rhino Territory Necessities**

   Rather than the more friendly White Rhino, the Dark Rhino shows a more single way of life and adjusts to a different scope of territories. Dark Rhinos can be tracked down in savannas, meadows, thick shrublands, and even deserts. Their snared upper lip is specific for perusing on leaves and twigs from shrubberies and trees, permitting them to take advantage of a more extensive scope of vegetation contrasted with their nibbler partners.

   The protection challenge for Dark Rhinos lies in safeguarding the range of living spaces they possess. This incorporates safeguarding savannas, guaranteeing the accessibility of browseable vegetation in shrublands, and tending to the infringement of human exercises in their living spaces. Against poaching endeavors are significant, as the singular idea of Dark Rhinos makes them more defenseless to unlawful hunting.

3. **Indian Rhino Territory Necessities**

   The Indian Rhino, otherwise called the More noteworthy One-Horned Rhino, is adjusted to damp prairies and woodlands. Semi-sea-going in nature, Indian Rhinos frequently occupy regions with water bodies like streams, marshes, and lakes. Their single horn recognizes them, and their skin, embellished with folds, gives an extraordinary appearance.

The preservation center for Indian Rhinos includes the assurance of their damp territories and the support of water sources. These regions are defenseless against living space corruption and human-untamed life struggle, accentuating the requirement for maintainable administration rehearses. Preservation drives likewise expect to address the double idea of Indian Rhino conduct, integrating techniques for both single and social associations.

4. **Javan Rhino Natural surroundings Prerequisites**

The Javan Rhino, one of the most uncommon and most jeopardized rhino species, lean towards thick tropical and subtropical woodlands. Their little and minimized form permits them to explore through the thick vegetation of their natural surroundings. Javan Rhinos are known for their subtle and singular way of behaving, mentioning direct observable facts testing.

Protection endeavors for the Javan Rhino center around safeguarding and reestablishing their woods natural surroundings. The thick idea of these environments expects measures to address natural surroundings discontinuity, guaranteeing network between various woodland patches. Hostile to poaching measures are especially basic, given the weakness of this species to unlawful hunting.

5. **Sumatran Rhino Environment Prerequisites**

The Sumatran Rhino, the littlest living rhino species, occupies thick tropical and subtropical backwoods. Not at all like other rhino species, Sumatran Rhinos have hair, giving them a shaggy appearance. With two horns and a singular nature, they scavenge for an assortment of vegetation, adding to the biodiversity of their timberland territory.

Preserving Sumatran Rhinos requires the insurance and reclamation of their forested surroundings. The thick vegetation presents difficulties for checking and research, requiring inventive preservation draws near. Given their lone way of behaving, understanding their development designs and laying out compelling enemy of poaching measures are vital for the endurance of this species.

Protection Suggestions and Difficulties

Protecting Living space Network: Territory fracture is a critical worry for rhino populaces. It upsets the network between various patches of reasonable territory, restricting the development of rhinos and separating populaces. Preservation methodologies should address the requirement for passages that work with quality stream, taking into account solid and hereditarily assorted populaces.

Human-Natural life Compromise: As human populaces grow, clashes among rhinos and nearby networks heighten. Crop harm and incidental showdowns present dangers to the two rhinos and individuals. Carrying out techniques for alleviating human-natural life struggle, for example, laying out support zones, presenting elective jobs, and utilizing innovation for early advance notice frameworks, is significant for cultivating conjunction.

Maintainable Administration Practices: Protection endeavors should consolidate supportable administration rehearses that balance the necessities of nearby networks with the prerequisites of rhino environments. This includes advancing dependable the travel industry, reasonable asset use, and local area based protection drives that engage nearby inhabitants to become stewards of their regular habitat.

Environmental Change Variation: The ramifications of environmental change represent extra difficulties for rhino territories. Changes in temperature and precipitation examples can influence vegetation conveyance, water accessibility, and in general living space appropriateness. Protection methodologies need to incorporate versatile measures to assist rhino populaces with adapting to the evolving environment, for example, establishing environment strong hallways and checking living space changes.

2.3 Interaction with Other Species in their Ecosystem

The connections among rhinos and different species inside their environments are essential parts of the complicated snare of life. As cornerstone species and biological system engineers, rhinos assume an essential part in molding their territories, impacting vegetation elements, and encouraging biodiversity. This article investigates the different and interconnected connections rhinos lay out with different creatures, going from mutualistic coordinated efforts to concurrence challenges. By understanding these collaborations, we gain bits of knowledge into the more extensive environmental meaning of rhinos and the protection suggestions for their cohabitating species.

1. **Cornerstone Species and Biological system Designing**
1. **Rhinos as Cornerstone Species**

   Rhinos, perceived as cornerstone species, apply lopsided impacts on their environments comparative with their overflow. Their impact reaches out past their immediate cooperations, molding the design and working of whole environments. Cornerstone species assume a urgent part in keeping up with biodiversity, and the decay of rhino populaces can include flowing impacts on different species inside their territories.
2. **Environment Designing by Rhinos**

Rhinos take part in biological system designing through their taking care of, floundering, and touching ways of behaving. The specific benefiting from vegetation forestalls the strength of specific plant species, advancing biodiversity. Floundering makes mud dejections that act as fundamental water hotspots for various species, especially during dry seasons. The fragrance checking of domains impacts the way of behaving of different creatures inside the environment, making a dynamic and interconnected local area.

II. Mutualistic Associations with Birds and Bugs

1. **Oxpeckers and Rhinos**
   One of the most notable mutualistic connections including rhinos is their relationship with oxpeckers, explicitly the Red-charged and Yellow-charged Oxpeckers. These birds go about as harmonious accomplices by roosting on rhinos and benefiting from ticks, parasites, and dead skin. Consequently, rhinos get prepping administrations that add to their general wellbeing. This mutualistic relationship grandstands how various species can coincide, each profiting from the presence of the other.
2. **Bugs and Rhinos**

Bugs likewise assume a part in the mutualistic cooperations with rhinos. Certain types of bugs, like creepy crawlies and parasites, use rhino fertilizer as a supplement rich substrate for their eggs. The disintegration of fertilizer adds to supplement cycling in the biological system, advancing soil wellbeing and vegetation development. Moreover, fertilizer scarabs assist with controlling fly populaces, by implication helping rhinos by diminishing the annoyance of parasitic bugs.

III. Interspecies Contest and Conjunction

1. **Contest with Elephants for Assets**
   Rhinos frequently share their natural surroundings with other huge herbivores, including elephants. The two species have covering dietary inclinations, making a potential for interspecies contest for assets like water and favored vegetation. Understanding the elements of this opposition is pivotal for compelling environment the board and preservation. Procedures that guarantee the accessibility of different assets can add to the concurrence of rhinos and elephants.
2. **Conjunction Difficulties with Animals**

In regions where rhino natural surroundings cross-over with human settlements and domesticated animals brushing, provokes emerge because of likely struggles. Rivalry for brushing lands, natural surroundings discontinuity, and the gamble of illness transmission between homegrown domesticated animals and rhinos present dangers to both rhino populaces and neighborhood livelihoods. Executing measures for practical land use, local area commitment, and sickness the executives is fundamental for encouraging concurrence.

IV. Predation Chance and Transformations

1. **Restricted Predation on Rhinos**
   Rhinos, as enormous herbivores, by and large face insignificant predation risk from regular hunters. Their size, strength, and imposing horns act as hindrances to most carnivores. In any case, youthful calves might be powerless against predation by enormous hunters like lions and hyenas. The shortfall of huge

predation pressure permits rhinos to zero in on keeping up with their regions, imitating, and adding to the by and large environmental equilibrium.

2. **Rhino Variations to Limit Predation Chance**

Transformative variations have furnished rhinos with highlights that limit predation risk. Their hard skin gives insurance against chomps and scratches, and the horns go about as considerable weapons against expected dangers.

Rhinos' sharp feeling of hearing and smell further upgrades their capacity to identify hunters, adding to their general step by step processes for surviving in nature.

V. Preservation Suggestions and Human-Untamed life Struggle

1. **Preservation Methodologies for Cornerstone Species**
   The protection of rhinos requires an extensive comprehension of their cooperations with different species. Safeguarding rhinos as cornerstone species includes saving their natural surroundings, overseeing interspecies rivalry, and tending to human-untamed life struggle. Preservation drives ought to think about the more extensive biological ramifications of rhino protection, perceiving the interconnected connections that support environments.

2. **Alleviating Human-Untamed life Struggle**

Human-natural life struggle emerges when the interests of neighborhood networks conflict with the presence of rhinos. Infringement on rhino environments, crop harm, and intermittent showdowns present difficulties for the two rhinos and individuals. Moderating clash includes carrying out techniques, for example, local area based preservation, making cradle zones, presenting elective jobs, and utilizing innovation for early advance notice frameworks.

VI. Environmental Change and Biological Elements

1. **Environmental Change Effect on Communications**
   The apparition of environmental change acquaints new elements with the associations inside biological systems. Changes in temperature, precipitation examples, and vegetation dispersion can influence the accessibility of assets for rhinos and their cohabitating species. Preservation techniques need to adjust to these changes, integrating environment versatile methodologies that think about the advancing natural scene.

2. **Worldwide Joint effort for Environment Versatile Protection**

Tending to the effects of environmental change on rhino natural surroundings requires worldwide cooperation. Associations like Refers to (Show on Global Exchange Jeopardized Types of Wild Fauna and Verdure) assume an essential part in working with worldwide collaboration. By sharing information, assets, and protection techniques, the worldwide local area can pursue environment tough preservation rehearses that benefit rhinos as well as the whole biological system.

Chapter 3

The Ecological Web

The biological web is a huge and multifaceted embroidery of connections that characterizes life on The planet. From minuscule living beings to transcending trees, each part of the regular world is complicatedly connected, shaping a perplexing organization of collaborations. This article dives into the different features of the natural web, looking at the association of species, the progression of energy, supplement cycling, and the significant effects of human exercises on this fragile equilibrium. As we unwind the complexities of the biological web, we gain a more profound comprehension of the significance of protection and economical practices for the soundness of our planet.

1. **The Interconnectedness of Species**
1. **Biotic Collaborations**
   The underpinning of the biological web lies in the biotic cooperations among species. These collaborations can be ordered into different classifications, including advantageous interaction, rivalry, predation, and mutualism. Advantageous connections, for example, the mutualistic connection between blooming plants and pollinators, represent the interconnectedness that describes environments. Essentially, the cutthroat elements between species for restricted assets drive the variation and development of creatures.
2. **Cornerstone Species**

Certain species, known as cornerstone species, altogether affect their biological systems. The expulsion of a cornerstone animal groups can prompt flowing impacts, disturbing the whole local area structure. Wolves in Yellowstone Public Park, for instance, go about as cornerstone hunters that manage herbivore populaces, impacting vegetation and in any event, adjusting the progression of streams. Understanding and rationing cornerstone species are fundamental for keeping up with the respectability of the natural web.

II. Energy Stream in Biological systems

1. **Trophic Levels and Food Networks**
Energy courses through biological systems in a unidirectional way, beginning with essential makers and advancing through different trophic levels. Essential makers, fundamentally plants, outfit energy from the sun through photosynthesis.
Herbivores consume plants, and carnivores feed on herbivores, making a progressive design known as trophic levels. The mind boggling examples of energy move and utilization structure food networks that delineate the interconnected connections inside biological systems.

2. **Energy Pyramids**

Energy pyramids portray the diminishing energy accessible at each trophic level. As energy is moved, a significant sum is lost as intensity during metabolic cycles. This peculiarity, known as the 10% rule, features the shortcoming of energy move between trophic levels. Subsequently, biological systems can uphold less top hunters because of the diminishing energy accessible as one climbs the pyramid.

III. Supplement Cycling and Biogeochemical Cycles

1. **Significance of Supplement Cycling**
Supplement cycling is a key interaction in the biological web, guaranteeing the accessibility of fundamental components like carbon, nitrogen, and phosphorus for living creatures. Decomposers, like microbes and parasites, make light of a basic job in breaking natural matter, returning supplements to the dirt for take-up by plants. This repeating system supports the equilibrium of supplements inside biological systems and impacts the efficiency of both earthly and amphibian conditions.

2. **Carbon Cycle**
The carbon cycle is a noticeable biogeochemical cycle with significant ramifications for environment guideline. Photosynthesis by plants and green growth assimilates carbon dioxide from the air, changing over it into natural mixtures. Breath, deterioration, and burning delivery carbon back into the air. Human exercises, especially the consuming of non-renewable energy sources, have fundamentally modified the carbon cycle, adding to environmental change.

3. **Nitrogen Cycle**

Nitrogen, a fundamental part of amino acids and nucleic acids, goes through a mind boggling cycle including nitrogen obsession, nitrification, denitrification, and ammonification. Microbes assume key parts in these cycles, working with the transformation of nitrogen between different structures. Human exercises, for example, the extreme utilization of nitrogen-based composts, can disturb the nitrogen cycle, prompting natural issues like water contamination.

IV. Human Effect on the Biological Web

1. **Environment Annihilation and Discontinuity**
   Human exercises, including deforestation, urbanization, and agribusiness, significantly affect the biological web. Environment annihilation and discontinuity upset biological systems, prompting the deficiency of biodiversity and the removal of species. The discontinuity of living spaces detaches populaces, lessening hereditary variety and blocking the normal progression of species across scenes.

2. **Contamination and Tainting**
   The arrival of contaminations into air, water, and soil presents extreme dangers to the biological web. Modern contaminations, farming spillover, and plastic waste negatively influence biological systems, causing environment corruption and compromising the wellbeing of various species. The amassing of poisons in food networks can prompt biomagnification, where higher trophic levels experience more prominent groupings of contaminations.

3. **Environmental Change**

Human-prompted environmental change is a worldwide test with broad ramifications for the biological web. Climbing temperatures, changed precipitation examples, and outrageous climate occasions upset biological systems, influencing the appropriation and conduct of species. Numerous creatures face moves in adjusting to the quickly evolving environment, prompting shifts in the organization of biological systems.

V. Preservation and Reclamation Endeavors

1. **Safeguarding Biodiversity**
   Preservation endeavors intend to moderate the effects of human exercises on the environmental web. Safeguarded regions, untamed life stores, and preservation drives assume urgent parts in saving biodiversity. Techniques incorporate natural surroundings rebuilding, renewed introduction programs for jeopardized species, and the foundation of hallways to reconnect divided living spaces.

2. **Maintainable Asset The executives**
   Feasible practices are significant for limiting the natural impression of human exercises. Feasible farming, fisheries the board, and capable ranger service rehearses expect to keep up with environment wellbeing while at the same time addressing human requirements. The reception of sustainable power sources and eco-accommodating advancements adds to lessening the natural effect of energy creation.

3. Environmental Change Relief and Transformation

Addressing environmental change requires worldwide endeavors to decrease ozone harming substance emanations and progress to supportable practices. Moderation systems center around limiting the reasons for environmental change, while transformation estimates expect to assist environments and species with adapting to the evolving environment. Peaceful accords, like the Paris Understanding, embody cooperative drives to handle environment related difficulties.

VI. The Job of Schooling and Promotion

1. Bringing issues to light

Schooling and promotion assume fundamental parts in cultivating a more profound comprehension of the natural web and the significance of protection. Natural schooling programs, outreach drives, and media crusades add to bringing issues to light about the interconnectedness of species, the results of human activities, and the direness of taking on supportable practices.

2. Local area Commitment

Drawing in neighborhood networks in protection endeavors is fundamental for the progress of environmental reclamation and conservation. Local area based protection programs engage inhabitants to become stewards of their indigenous habitats, adjusting preservation objectives to nearby interests and cultivating a feeling of shared liability regarding the prosperity of environments.

3.1 Overview of Ecosystem Interactions

Biological systems, the multifaceted organizations of living creatures and their actual surroundings, are portrayed by a huge number of collaborations that shape the elements of life on The planet. This exposition gives a thorough outline of biological system collaborations, investigating the different connections between creatures, the progression of energy, supplement cycling, and the more extensive effects of these communications on the wellbeing and manageability of environments. As we dig into the intricacies of these connections, we gain a more profound comprehension of the crucial rules that oversee the working and versatility of environments.

1. Biotic Collaborations: The Core of Environment Elements

1. Beneficial interaction

Advantageous collaborations structure the groundwork of biodiversity inside environments. Beneficial interaction envelops a range of connections, including mutualism, where both cooperating species benefit; commensalism, where one advantages while the other is unaffected; and parasitism, where one advantages to the detriment of the other.

Models have large amounts of nature, for example, the mutualistic connection between blooming plants and pollinators, the commensal connection among barnacles and whales, and the parasitic connection among ticks and warm blooded animals.

2. **Contest and Asset Apportioning**

   Contest for assets, like daylight, water, and supplements, is a main impetus in biological systems. Species develop components to parcel assets, decreasing direct contest and advancing conjunction. Asset parceling can appear in transient, spatial, or morphological variations, permitting species with comparable biological specialties to flourish inside a similar environment. This cycle adds to the rich variety saw in different environmental networks.

3. **Predation and Herbivory**

Predation and herbivory are fundamental biological cycles that manage populaces inside environments. Hunters apply hierarchical control on prey populaces, affecting their dispersion and conduct. Likewise, herbivores influence plant networks, molding vegetation structure and affecting the piece of environments. Trophic fountains, where changes in one trophic level effect others, delineate the interconnectedness of hunter prey connections.

II. Trophic Design and Energy Stream

1. **Trophic Levels and Food Networks**

   Trophic levels address the progressive design of taking care of connections inside biological systems. Essential makers, commonly plants and green growth, possess the first trophic level, trailed by herbivores, carnivores, and dominant hunters. Food networks portray the mind boggling and interconnected pathways through which energy streams as living beings devour and are eaten by others. These networks feature the significance of both immediate and aberrant communications in supporting the equilibrium of biological systems.

2. **Energy Move and the 10% Rule**

The progression of energy through trophic levels is dependent upon the 10% rule, where just roughly 10% of energy is moved starting with one trophic level then onto the next. This standard mirrors the shortcoming of energy move in natural frameworks, underlining the significance of essential makers in outfitting sun powered energy through photosynthesis. Understanding energy elements is significant for anticipating the effects of unsettling influences on environments and overseeing assets reasonably.

III. Supplement Cycling and Biogeochemical Cycles

1. **Supplement Cycling in Environments**

   Supplement cycling includes the constant development and reusing of fundamental components, like carbon, nitrogen, phosphorus, and sulfur, inside environments. Decomposers make light of a basic job in breaking natural matter, delivering supplements into the dirt for take-up by plants. Supplement cycling guarantees the accessibility of these components for different creatures, impacting the efficiency and wellbeing of biological systems.

2. **Carbon Cycle**

   The carbon cycle, a major biogeochemical cycle, envelops cycles like photosynthesis, breath, decay, and burning. Human exercises, especially the consuming of petroleum derivatives, have disturbed the normal equilibrium of the carbon cycle, prompting raised air carbon dioxide levels and adding to environmental change. Dealing with the carbon cycle is fundamental for moderating the effects of worldwide natural change.

3. **Nitrogen Cycle**

The nitrogen cycle includes the change of barometrical nitrogen into structures that plants can use. Nitrogen obsession, nitrification, denitrification, and ammonification are key cycles worked with by different microorganisms. Human-incited exercises, for example, the unreasonable utilization of nitrogen-based composts, can prompt nitrogen contamination, influencing water quality and biological system wellbeing. Adjusting the nitrogen cycle is basic for economical horticulture and protection.

IV. Aggravations and Environmental Versatility

1. **Regular and Anthropogenic Aggravations**

   Biological systems are dependent upon aggravations, both normal and anthropogenic, that impact their construction and organization. Normal unsettling influences, like rapidly spreading fires, floods, and tropical storms, are necessary to environment elements, molding successional designs and advancing biodiversity. Anthropogenic aggravations, including deforestation, contamination, and urbanization, can upset biological systems and challenge their versatility.

2. **Progression and Variation**

   Natural progression is the course of steady change in the structure of an environment over the long run. Essential progression happens on recently shaped surfaces, while auxiliary progression follows aggravations that don't kill all life. Trailblazer species, portrayed by their capacity to colonize fruitless conditions, prepare for additional mind boggling networks. Understanding progression is urgent for biological system rebuilding and protection.

3. **Biological Versatility and Strength**

Flexibility is the limit of an environment to retain unsettling influences and rearrange while keeping up with fundamental capabilities. Environment soundness, then again, alludes to the capacity to oppose variances and return to a decent state.

Biodiversity, overt repetitiveness, and utilitarian variety add to versatility and dependability. Human exercises that dissolve flexibility, for example, living space obliteration and environmental change, present difficulties for keeping up with solid and manageable biological systems.

V. Human Effect on Biological system Connections

1. **Natural surroundings Annihilation and Fracture**

   Human exercises, driven by populace development and industrialization, have prompted far and wide environment obliteration and fracture. This interruption modifies the accessibility of assets, separates populaces, and compromises biodiversity. Preservation endeavors center around relieving these effects through environment rebuilding, safeguarded regions, and reasonable land-use rehearses.

2. **Contamination and Defilement**

   Contamination, including air, water, and soil contamination, presents serious dangers to biological systems. Synthetic toxins from modern and farming sources can disturb supplement cycling, hurt oceanic life, and compromise air quality. Alleviating contamination includes administrative measures, reasonable practices, and the improvement of innovations that diminish ecological effect.

3. **Environmental Change**

Human-instigated environmental change is a worldwide test that impacts biological system communications on a planetary scale. Increasing temperatures, adjusted precipitation examples, and outrageous climate occasions influence the circulation and conduct of species. Environments should adjust to these changes, and protection endeavors progressively center around environment strong practices and the decrease of ozone harming substance discharges.

VI. Preservation Methodologies and Feasible Practices

1. **Safeguarding Biodiversity**

   Biodiversity is vital for biological system wellbeing and strength. Preservation techniques include safeguarding normal natural surroundings, laying out untamed life hallways, and carrying out measures to forestall the eradication of imperiled species. The safeguarding of biodiversity adds to the versatile limit of biological systems despite ecological changes.

2. **Maintainable Asset The executives**

   Supportable practices in farming, ranger service, and fisheries plan to offset human asset use with environment wellbeing. Practices like natural cultivating, particular logging, and dependable fishing add to keeping up with the trustworthiness of biological systems. Reasonable asset the executives is fundamental for addressing human necessities while limiting natural effects.

3. **Reclamation and Restoration**

   Environment reclamation includes the deliberate adjustment of biological systems to restore their construction and capability. Rebuilding tasks might zero in on recuperating debased living spaces, once again introducing local species, and upgrading environment administrations. Recovery endeavors frequently include the expulsion of intrusive species and the advancement of regular recovery to improve environment flexibility.

4. **Local area Commitment and Instruction**

Drawing in neighborhood networks in protection endeavors is urgent for the progress of biological system safeguarding. Local area based protection programs engage inhabitants to become stewards of their common habitats, adjusting preservation objectives to neighborhood interests. Training drives bring issues to light about the significance of environments, encouraging a feeling of obligation for their security.

3.2Identification of Key Players in Rhino Ecosystems

Rhino biological systems are perplexing and dynamic conditions where different species assume key parts in molding the natural equilibrium. Recognizing the central participants inside these environments is critical for appreciating the reliance of species and creating compelling protection techniques. This paper investigates the huge supporters of rhino environments, going from megaherbivores and cornerstone species to minuscule living beings, underlining their interconnected jobs in supporting the wellbeing and usefulness of these extraordinary natural surroundings.

1. **Megaherbivores: The Modelers of Biological system Construction**

1. **Rhinos as Cornerstone Species**

   Rhinos, especially the White Rhino and Dark Rhino species, arise as cornerstone species inside their biological systems. As megaherbivores, they apply significant impact on vegetation elements through their taking care of propensities. The particular touching and perusing ways of behaving of rhinos shape the arrangement of plant networks, forestalling the strength of specific species and advancing biodiversity.

   Their floundering exercises make fundamental water hotspots for a large number of organic entities and add to soil richness. The protection of rhinos is necessary to saving the underlying trustworthiness and variety of their biological systems.

2. **Elephants as Environment Specialists**

Close by rhinos, elephants stand apart as impressive megaherbivores that engineer biological systems. Their perusing exercises impact vegetation structure, prompting the production of unmistakable territories. Elephants assume a crucial part in seed dispersal, helping with the recovery of plant species. Their effect on tree populaces can shape the savanna scene, showing their importance as biological system designers. Preservation endeavors for the two rhinos and elephants add to keeping up with the natural equilibrium of their common environments.

II. Mutualistic Associations: Oxpeckers and Rhinos

1. Oxpeckers as Mutualistic Partners

In the many-sided snare of connections inside rhino environments, oxpeckers (Red-charged and Yellow-charged Oxpeckers) lay out mutualistic organizations with rhinos. These birds feed on ticks, parasites, and dead skin, giving a prepping administration that benefits rhinos by advancing cleanliness and wellbeing. Consequently, oxpeckers get a solid wellspring of food. This mutualistic relationship grandstands the association of species and features the job of more modest organic entities in adding to the prosperity of bigger ones.

III. Soil Microorganisms: The Inconspicuous Stewards of Biological system Wellbeing

1. Job of Soil Microorganisms

Underneath the outer layer of rhino environments, a large number of soil microorganisms works as concealed stewards of biological system wellbeing. Microbes and growths assume basic parts in supplement cycling, decaying natural matter, and improving soil richness. Mycorrhizal organisms structure cooperative associations with plant roots, working with supplement take-up and advancing plant development. The variety and action of soil microorganisms add to the general strength and efficiency of rhino living spaces.

IV. Greenery Variety: Harmonious Connections and Living space Design

1. Plant Species Variety

The variety of plant species inside rhino environments adds to the general design and capability of these territories. Different plant species satisfy explicit jobs, from giving food to megaherbivores to making microhabitats for different creatures. Grasses, bushes, and trees each add to the many-sided mosaic of the scene.

Protection endeavors should address the conservation of different plant networks to support the dietary necessities of rhinos and the whole biological system.

2. Cooperative Associations with Plants

Certain plant species take part in advantageous associations with rhinos and other megaherbivores. For instance, acacia trees have developed thistles as a protection system against herbivores. Thus, programs like rhinos and elephants consume these prickly trees, profiting from their nourishing substance. This communication exhibits the coevolutionary elements among plants and megaherbivores, underlining the interconnected jobs they play in forming biological systems.

V. Hunters and Foragers: Directing Herbivore Populaces

1. **Hunters as Populace Controllers**

   Hunters inside rhino environments, like lions and hyenas, assume a urgent part in controlling herbivore populaces. By controlling the quantities of herbivores, hunters forestall overgrazing and keep a harmony among vegetation and creature populaces. The presence of hunters adds to the general wellbeing and versatility of the environment, forestalling the unrestrained extension of herbivore populaces that could prompt living space debasement.

2. **Scroungers and Decomposers**

Scroungers, including vultures and hyenas, add to the productive evacuation of cadavers inside rhino environments. Their job as decomposers speeds up the reusing of supplements, restoring natural make a difference to the dirt. This interaction upholds the supplement cycling instruments fundamental for the development of plants and supports the general soundness of the environment. The preservation of foragers is interlaced with the more extensive endeavors to protect the environmental equilibrium.

VI. Human People group: Coinciding with Rhino Environments

1. **Local area Based Protection**

   Human people group living in vicinity to rhino environments are essential players in the protection story. Local area based preservation drives include nearby occupants in enemy of poaching endeavors, environment rebuilding, and instructive projects. Drawing in networks as stewards of their common habitat adjusts protection objectives to neighborhood interests, cultivating a feeling of shared liability. Effective conjunction with rhino environments requires tending to the necessities of human networks while advancing supportable practices.

2. **The travel industry as a Protection Device**

The travel industry can act as a protection device by giving monetary impetuses to the conservation of rhino living spaces. Very much oversaw ecotourism adds to neighborhood economies, reserves protection drives, and brings issues to light about the significance of saving biodiversity. Adjusting the financial advantages of the travel industry with the security of rhino biological systems is fundamental for guaranteeing an amicable connection between human networks and these crucial environments.

VII. Preservation Difficulties and Future Contemplations

1. **Poaching and Unlawful Natural life Exchange**

   Poaching stays a huge danger to rhino populaces and their environments. The unlawful natural life exchange, driven by the interest for rhino horns, presents difficulties for preservation endeavors. Tending to these difficulties requires hearty enemy of poaching measures, worldwide cooperation, and endeavors to diminish interest for rhino items.

2. **Environment Misfortune and Fracture**

   Environment misfortune and fracture, driven by human exercises like farming and urbanization, upset rhino biological systems. Preservation procedures should address land-use arranging, the foundation of safeguarded regions, and drives to reestablish debased territories. Making associated scenes that take into account the normal development of rhinos and different species is urgent for keeping up with biological system usefulness.

3. **Environmental Change Effects**

Environmental change represents extra difficulties to rhino biological systems. Changes in temperature and precipitation designs, also as outrageous climate occasions, can influence vegetation appropriation and water accessibility. Preservation estimates need to integrate environment versatile techniques, for example, establishing environment halls and checking the versatile limit of biological systems to changing environment conditions.

3.3 Cascading Effects of Rhino Presence or Absence

The presence or nonappearance of rhinos inside environments sets off an outpouring of impacts that resonate through the perplexing trap of connections. As cornerstone species and megaherbivores, rhinos assume a urgent part in forming their living spaces. This exposition investigates the flowing impacts that unfurl when rhinos are available or missing, underscoring the interconnected elements that impact vegetation, other natural life, and in general biological system wellbeing.

1. **Flowing Impacts of Rhino Presence**
1. **Vegetation Elements and Biodiversity**

   At the point when rhinos are available in a biological system, their specific taking care of ways of behaving make a mosaic of vegetation. Rhinos are programs and slow eaters, consuming an assortment of plant animal types. By forestalling the strength of specific plants, they advance biodiversity and make great circumstances for a different scope of vegetation. The patches of vegetation made by rhino taking care of become safe houses for various plant species, affecting the general construction and sythesis of the environment.

2. **Seed Dispersal and Recovery**

   Rhinos additionally add to seed dispersal, especially through their excrement. Seeds from consumed plants go through the stomach related framework and are kept in various areas, supporting the recovery of plant species. This interaction is fundamental for the regular restoration of the biological system, guaranteeing the dispersal of seeds across shifted environments. The presence of rhinos consequently turns into a main thrust behind the recurrent recharging and variety of vegetation.

3. **Floundering and Water Sources**

   Rhinos participate in floundering conduct, making mud melancholies that act as fundamental water hotspots for different creatures. These mud flounders become central focuses for other untamed life, including birds, bugs, and more modest vertebrates. The presence of rhinos, consequently, adds to the accessibility of water in environments, supporting a different exhibit of life. The interconnectedness of rhinos with water sources features their job as environment engineers.

4. **Mutualistic Connections**

Rhinos structure mutualistic associations with oxpeckers, like the Red-charged and Yellow-charged Oxpeckers. These birds feed on ticks and parasites present on rhinos, giving a cleaning administration that benefits the two players. Rhinos gain help from parasites, while oxpeckers get a food source. The advantageous bond represents the interconnected connections cultivated by the presence of rhinos, adding to the general strength of the biological system.

II. Flowing Impacts of Rhino Nonattendance

1. **Adjusted Vegetation Elements**

   The shortfall of rhinos can prompt modified vegetation elements inside environments. Without the specific perusing and touching exercises of rhinos, certain plant species might become prevailing, possibly outcompeting others.

   This change in vegetation organization can affect the biodiversity of the environment, leaning toward certain species while smothering the development of others. The shortfall of rhinos upsets the normal equilibrium that their presence keeps up with.

2. **Diminished Seed Dispersal**

   The shortfall of rhinos means a decrease in seed dispersal. As megaherbivores, rhinos assume a pivotal part in scattering seeds through their excrement. Without rhinos, the dispersal of seeds becomes restricted, influencing the normal recovery of plant species. This decrease in seed dispersal can have flowing consequences for the development and appropriation of vegetation inside the environment.

3. **Decreased Water Sources**

   The shortfall of rhinos implies a decrease in floundering conduct and the formation of mud despondencies. This, thus, influences the accessibility of water hotspots for other natural life. Mud flounders made by rhinos are fundamental for their own utilization as well as act as basic water focuses for different creatures. The shortfall of rhinos can prompt difficulties for different species in getting to dependable water sources, especially during dry periods.

4. **Interruption of Mutualistic Connections**

Rhino nonattendance upsets the mutualistic connections they have with oxpeckers. Without rhinos as hosts, oxpeckers might confront difficulties in tracking down reasonable wellsprings of food. The break in this mutualistic bond can have ramifications for the two rhinos and oxpeckers, featuring the perplexing conditions that portray environments. The shortfall of one central participant can set off a chain response influencing various species.

III. Preservation Suggestions

1. **Rhino Preservation for Biological system Wellbeing**

   Understanding the flowing impacts of rhino presence or nonappearance accentuates the basic job of rhinos in keeping up with the wellbeing and usefulness of environments. Preservation endeavors should focus on the security of rhinos, remembering them as cornerstone species and biological system engineers. Saving rhino populaces includes tending to dangers like poaching, environment misfortune, and human-untamed life struggle to guarantee their proceeded with presence in their normal natural surroundings.

2. **All encompassing Biological system The board**

   Preservation techniques need to take on an all encompassing methodology that thinks about the more extensive ramifications of rhino protection. Safeguarding rhinos goes past shielding a solitary animal varieties; it includes saving the complex snare of connections and environmental cycles that characterize their biological systems. Comprehensive biological system the executives incorporates measures to address living space fracture, improve network, and advance feasible concurrence among rhinos and neighborhood networks.

3. **Teaching Partners**

Bringing issues to light about the flowing impacts of rhino presence or nonappearance is vital for collecting support for protection drives. Instructing nearby networks, policymakers, and the worldwide crowd about the interconnectedness of species inside biological systems cultivates a feeling of shared liability. Informed partners are bound to participate in endeavors that add to the conservation of rhinos and the more extensive biodiversity of their territories.

Chapter 4

Rhino-Mediated Landscape Changes

Rhinos, as megaherbivores and cornerstone species, apply a significant impact on the scenes they possess. This exposition investigates the unpredictable elements of rhino-interceded scene changes, diving into the biological effect of these lofty animals. From their scavenging ways of behaving and floundering exercises to their job in seed dispersal and vegetation elements, rhinos assume a urgent part in molding environments. Understanding the subtleties of rhino-interceded scene changes is fundamental for protection endeavors, as these animals explore dangers like poaching, living space misfortune, and human-untamed life struggle. This complete investigation expects to reveal insight into the complicated interchange among rhinos and their surroundings, underscoring the significance of safeguarding these megaherbivores for the wellbeing and strength of scenes.

1. **Presentation: The Cornerstone Job of Rhinos in Environments**
1. **Cornerstone Species Definition and Importance**
   Cornerstone species are those whose presence or nonappearance to a great extent affects their environments. Rhinos, having a place with both the White Rhino (Ceratotherium simum) and Dark Rhino (Diceros bicornis) species, encapsulate the pith of cornerstone species. Their importance lies in their capacity to shape scenes through different natural cycles, making them basic for the wellbeing and usefulness of their environments.
2. **Megaherbivores: The Designers of Environment Construction**

Rhinos, as megaherbivores, stand among the biggest herbivores on earth. Their size and taking care of propensities add to their job as planners of environment structure. By impacting vegetation elements, supplement cycling, and water accessibility, rhinos shape the scenes they occupy. This segment makes way for an itemized investigation of how rhinos intervene changes in scenes.

II. Scrounging Ways of behaving and Vegetation Elements

1. **Specific Brushing and Perusing Examples**
   Rhinos display particular searching ways of behaving, consolidating both touching and perusing exercises. Their particular taking care of examples significantly affect the creation and circulation of plant species inside their natural surroundings. Understanding the subtleties of these ways of behaving gives bits of knowledge into how rhinos impact vegetation elements.

2. **Influence on Plant Species Variety**
   Rhinos assume a vital part in keeping up with plant species variety. Through their particular taking care of, they forestall the predominance of explicit plant species, setting out open doors for different plants to coincide. This variety adds to the general flexibility of biological systems, improving their capacity to endure natural changes.

3. **Vegetation Design and Living space Heterogeneity**

The scrounging exercises of rhinos add to the underlying intricacy and heterogeneity of vegetation. By making open spaces through touching and altering the design of vegetation through perusing, rhinos impact the accessibility of assets for different species. This part investigates how rhinos shape the actual scene through their communications with plants.

III. Floundering Exercises and Water Sources

1. **Floundering as Biological system Designing**
   Rhinos participate in floundering conduct, making mud dejections in the scene. These flounders act as something beyond places for rhinos to chill; they go about as fundamental water hotspots for various creatures. Floundering has environment designing impacts, affecting the accessibility of water for both natural life and more modest living beings inside the biological system.

2. **Microhabitat Creation and Soil Richness**

Floundering exercises make microhabitats that encourage exceptional environmental circumstances. The dampness from flounders advances the development of explicit plant species, adding to restricted biodiversity. Also, the mud from flounders improves soil ripeness, affecting supplement cycling and helping vegetation in the encompassing regions.

IV. Seed Dispersal and Plant Recovery

1. **Rhino as Seed Dispersers**
   Rhinos assume a critical part in seed dispersal through their utilization of products of the soil. The seeds go through the stomach related framework and are kept in various areas, helping with the recovery of plant species. This part

digs into the systems of rhino-interceded seed dispersal and its suggestions for plant variety.

2. **Regular Recovery and Scene Restoration**

The course of seed dispersal by rhinos adds to the regular recovery of vegetation. The foundation of new plants and the repeating recharging of scenes are results of rhino-intervened seed dispersal. This segment investigates how rhinos effectively partake in forming the structure and appropriation of plant networks.

V. Mutualistic Connections and Interconnected Web

1. **Oxpeckers and Rhinos: A Mutualistic Bond**
Rhinos structure mutualistic associations with oxpeckers, especially the Red-charged and Yellow-charged Oxpeckers. These birds feed on ticks and parasites present on rhinos, giving a cleaning administration that benefits the two players. This segment investigates the elements of this harmonious bond and its suggestions for the prosperity of rhinos and oxpeckers.

2. **Interconnected Connections in Environments**

The mutualistic connections including rhinos feature the interconnectedness of species inside environments. The prosperity of one animal categories can have flowing impacts on others, underscoring the mind boggling trap of connections that describes solid biological systems. This part explains the more extensive ramifications of interconnected connections in rhino-occupied scenes.

VI. Human-Untamed life Struggle and Preservation Difficulties

1. **Poaching as a Danger to Rhino Populaces**
Notwithstanding their biological importance, rhinos face various dangers, with poaching being an essential concern. The unlawful exchange rhino horns keeps on devastating populaces, representing an extreme test to preservation endeavors. This segment examines the effect of poaching on rhino populaces and the ensuing disturbance of their environmental jobs.

2. **Environment Misfortune and Fracture**
Human exercises, including environment misfortune and fracture, further undermine rhino populaces. Urbanization, farming, and foundation advancement infringe upon rhino territories, prompting natural surroundings corruption and seclusion.
Preservation systems should address these difficulties to guarantee the proceeded with presence of rhinos in scenes.

3. **Human-Natural life Struggle Relief**

Conjunction among rhinos and human networks is pivotal for preservation achievement. Human-natural life struggle, including cases of yield striking and experiences with rhinos, requires successful moderation techniques. This segment investigates ways to deal with cultivating amicability between human networks and rhinos, recognizing the significance of neighborhood commitment in preservation.

VII. Protection Techniques for Rhino-Interceded Scenes

1. **Safeguarded Regions and Protection Stores**
   Laying out and keeping up with safeguarded regions and protection saves are fundamental for defending rhino territories. This segment digs into the significance of making spaces where rhinos can flourish, liberated from the prompt dangers of poaching and environment obliteration.

2. **Local area Based Preservation Drives**
   Connecting with neighborhood networks in protection endeavors is principal for the outcome of rhino preservation. Local area based drives engage inhabitants to become stewards of their regular habitat, encouraging a feeling of shared liability. This part investigates the job of local area based preservation in saving rhino-interceded scenes.

3. **Movement and Renewed introduction Projects**

Movement and renewed introduction programs assume a basic part in reestablishing rhino populaces in regions where they have been extirpated. This part talks about the difficulties and advantages of such projects, featuring their commitment to upgrading rhino-intervened scene changes.

VIII. Future Viewpoints and Exploration Headings

1. **Mechanical Developments in Rhino Preservation**
   Progressions in innovation, including satellite following, DNA examination, and against poaching measures, offer new roads for rhino protection. This segment investigates how mechanical advancements can add to more viable preservation techniques and observing endeavors.

2. **Research Holes and Environmental Comprehension**

Notwithstanding progress in rhino protection, there are still holes in our biological comprehension of their jobs in scenes. This segment recognizes key examination regions and questions that need investigation to upgrade how we might interpret rhino-intervened scene changes.

4.1 Rhino Grazing and Its Impact on Vegetation
Rhino touching is a crucial biological cycle that impacts vegetation elements in the scenes they possess. This article investigates the perplexing connection between rhino brushing and vegetation, digging into the specific taking care of ways of behaving of

rhinos, their effect on plant networks, and the more extensive environmental ramifications. From the job of rhinos as megaherbivores to their impact on plant species variety and natural surroundings structure, understanding the subtleties of rhino brushing is fundamental for fathoming the biological elements of the environments they shape. Protection endeavors should consider the fragile harmony between rhino populaces and vegetation wellbeing to guarantee the versatility and maintainability of these exceptional natural surroundings.

1. **Presentation: Rhino Touching as a Natural Cycle**
1. **Job of Megaherbivores in Biological systems**
   Megaherbivores, described by their enormous size and herbivorous eating routine, assume an essential part in molding environments. Rhinos, as conspicuous megaherbivores, contribute essentially to vegetation elements through their brushing exercises. This segment makes way for a nitty gritty investigation of what rhino brushing means for vegetation and the flowing consequences for biological system wellbeing.
2. **Meaning of Rhino Touching in Environment Usefulness**

Understanding the meaning of rhino touching requires an enthusiasm for its natural ramifications. Rhino populaces, made out of both White Rhinos (Ceratotherium simum) and Dark Rhinos (Diceros bicornis), have advanced to fill explicit specialties in their living spaces. Rhino brushing isn't simply a taking care of conduct however a powerful biological cycle that shapes the piece, design, and versatility of environments.

II. Rhino Taking care of Ways of behaving: A Mix of Touching and Perusing

1. **Touching and Perusing Characterized**
   Rhinos show a mix of brushing and perusing ways of behaving, recognizing them as blended feeders. Nibbling includes the utilization of grasses, while perusing involves benefiting from bushes, shrubs, and even trees. The flexibility of rhino taking care of ways of behaving empowers them to take advantage of an extensive variety of plant species, adding to their biological versatility.
2. **Particular Taking care of and Its Suggestions**
   Rhinos are particular feeders, showing inclinations for specific plant species over others. This specific taking care of conduct includes significant ramifications for the vegetation inside their natural surroundings. By picking explicit plants for utilization, rhinos impact the overflow, conveyance, and sythesis of plant networks, adding to the mosaic-like construction of their environments.
3. **Constantly Taking care of Examples**

Rhinos show unmistakable taking care of examples during various times. Night-time taking care of is normal, permitting rhinos to keep away from the intensity of the day. Understanding these taking care of examples gives experiences into the worldly elements of rhino brushing and its effect on vegetation over diurnal and occasional cycles.

III. Influence on Vegetation Elements

1. **Forestalling Predominance: Keeping up with Plant Variety**
   Rhino touching forestalls the strength of specific plant species inside their environments. By specifically consuming vegetation, rhinos set out open doors for a different exhibit of plant species to coincide. This variety is fundamental for biological system strength, as various plants contribute exceptional natural capabilities and adjust to fluctuating ecological circumstances.

2. **Making Open Spaces and Natural surroundings Heterogeneity**
   The demonstration of brushing itself adds to natural surroundings heterogeneity. Rhinos make open spaces inside the scene through their touching exercises. These open spaces impact the accessibility of assets for different species and add to the primary intricacy of the biological system. The interchange between rhino touching and territory heterogeneity is pivotal for supporting an assortment of natural life.

3. **Impact on Plant Populaces and Progression**

Rhino brushing impacts plant populaces and successional elements. Certain plant species might be leaned toward or smothered in light of their satisfactoriness to rhinos. The effect on plant populaces adds to successional designs, forming the general direction of vegetation changes after some time.

IV. Soil Fruitfulness, Supplement Cycling, and Water Accessibility

1. **Rhino Compost as a Wellspring of Supplements**
   Rhino manure fills in as a supplement rich asset that adds to soil ripeness. As rhinos brush and peruse, they store manure across the scene, delivering fundamental supplements into the dirt.
   This segment investigates the job of rhino manure in giving a supplement sponsorship that impacts the development and wellbeing of vegetation.

2. **Improved Supplement Cycling and Decay**
   The presence of rhinos improves supplement cycling inside environments. Their manure draws in a different local area of decomposers, including bugs and microorganisms, speeding up the decay of natural matter. This improved supplement cycling benefits vegetation by making fundamental supplements all the more promptly accessible for plant take-up.

3. **Water Accessibility from Floundering Exercises**

Floundering, one more way of behaving related with rhinos, adds to water accessibility inside environments. Rhino flounders, made by the blending of mud and water, become central focuses for other natural life and give fundamental water sources during dry periods. The interconnected elements of rhino ways of behaving, including brushing and floundering, impact the general water accessibility in their environments.

V. Difficulties and Variations Despite Human-Incited Changes

1. **Human-Natural life Struggle: Harvest Attacking and Environment Discontinuity**

   As human populaces grow, rhinos frequently clash with rural exercises, prompting cases of yield attacking. Living space fracture because of human improvement further difficulties rhino populaces. This segment investigates what these human-incited changes mean for rhino brushing ways of behaving and their versatile reactions.

2. **Changed Taking care of Ways of behaving in Human-Overwhelmed Scenes**

In scenes where human exercises have changed regular environments, rhinos might display adjusted taking care of ways of behaving. This variation could include changes in dietary inclinations, timing of taking care of exercises, or adjustments in the utilization of accessible assets. Understanding these variations is urgent for creating protection methodologies that advance concurrence in human-overwhelmed scenes.

VI. Protection Suggestions and Methodologies

1. **Safeguarding Rhino-Interceded Brushing Examples for Biological system Wellbeing**

   Protection endeavors should focus on the safeguarding of rhino-interceded brushing examples to keep up with environment wellbeing. This segment examines the ramifications of disturbed rhino touching for vegetation elements and the more extensive environment. It underlines the significance of relieving dangers, for example, poaching and living space misfortune to guarantee the proceeded with job of rhinos as natural planners.

2. **All encompassing Biological system The executives and Environment Reclamation**

   Comprehensive environment the executives includes tending to the more extensive natural setting in which rhinos exist. Systems might incorporate living space reclamation, making untamed life passageways, and overseeing scenes to help the regular ways of behaving of rhinos. This part investigates the job of all encompassing methodologies in encouraging sound biological systems.

3. **Local area Commitment and Practical Concurrence**

Drawing in neighborhood networks in protection endeavors is essential for the outcome of rhino safeguarding. This includes encouraging a comprehension of the environmental job of rhinos, tending to human-untamed life struggle, and incorporating supportable concurrence rehearses. The paper features effective local area based preservation drives that adjust protection objectives to the necessities and viewpoints of neighborhood occupants.

VII. Future Exploration Bearings and Logical Advancements

1. **Progressions in Following and Checking Rhino Conduct**
   Mechanical developments, like satellite following and remote detecting, offer new roads for checking rhino conduct. This segment investigates how these headways add to a more complete comprehension of rhino brushing designs and their natural effect.

2. **Environmental Change and Its Suggestions for Rhino Touching**

Environmental change presents difficulties to biological systems, affecting elements like vegetation development, water accessibility, and temperature designs. This segment examines the expected ramifications of environmental change on rhino brushing ways of behaving and investigates roads for adjusting preservation systems to an evolving environment.

4.2 Soil Composition Changes Due to Rhino Activities
The Biological Meaning of Rhino-Soil Associations

1. **Megaherbivores as Environment Designers**
   Megaherbivores, including rhinos, are perceived as environment engineers because of their capacity to shape the physical and natural attributes of their living spaces. This part accentuates the job of rhinos in affecting soil organization and features the interconnected connection between rhino exercises and soil elements.

2. **Soil as a Pivotal Part of Biological system Wellbeing**

Soil fills in as an essential part of earthbound biological systems, assuming an imperative part in supporting plant development, supplement cycling, and water maintenance. Changes in soil sythesis, driven by rhino exercises, have extensive ramifications for the wellbeing and usefulness of environments.

II. Rhino Excrement as a Supplement Source

1. **Supplement Rich Attributes of Rhino Excrement**
   Rhino excrement is a powerful wellspring of supplements that fundamentally adds to soil fruitfulness. The organization of rhino manure incorporates natural

matter, minerals, and undigested plant material, making a supplement rich substrate that impacts soil creation upon statement.

2. **Decay Cycles and Supplement Cycling**
Upon testimony, rhino manure goes through decay processes worked with by a different local area of decomposers, including bugs, organisms, and micro-organisms. This deterioration prompts the arrival of supplements into the dirt, adding to fundamental cycles like supplement cycling.

3. **Influence on Soil Construction and Microbial People group**

The presence of rhino waste impacts soil structure by upgrading total and advancing microbial action. The communication between compost related microorganisms and soil organisms adds to the general wellbeing and versatility of the dirt environment.

III. Floundering Conduct: Making Microhabitats and Upgrading Soil Richness

1. **Floundering as Biological system Designing**
Floundering, a way of behaving showed by rhinos, includes the formation of mud dejections by blending soil in with water. These flounders act as micro-habitats with extraordinary natural circumstances and have suggestions for soil ripeness and supplement accessibility.

2. **Microbial Variety in Flounder Conditions**
Flounder conditions encourage a rich variety of microorganisms, including microscopic organisms and growths. The blending of soil and water makes conditions helpful for microbial development, improving the microbial variety in these microhabitats.

3. **Supplement Improvement and Soil Dampness**

Floundering adds to supplement improvement in soils, as the mud in flounders contains natural matter from rhino skin and exudates. Furthermore, flounders up-grade soildampness maintenance, giving a confined wellspring of water for vegetation and adding to the making of dynamic microenvironments.

IV. Soil pH and Supplement Elements in Rhino-Impacted Conditions

1. **Rhino Manure and Soil pH**
The creation of rhino manure, including its basic nature, can impact soil pH in rhino-affected conditions. Changes in soil pH have flowing consequences for supplement accessibility, plant species piece, and microbial networks.

2. **Nitrogen Cycling and Plant Development**
Rhino excrement contains nitrogen, a critical supplement for plant develop-ment. The statement of nitrogen-rich compost adds to nitrogen cycling in

soils, impacting the accessibility of this fundamental supplement for plants and influencing the general efficiency of vegetation.

3. **Phosphorus Elements and Soil Richness**

Phosphorus, another essential supplement, is available in rhino waste in structures that can improve soil fruitfulness. The communication between rhino compost and soil phosphorus elements has suggestions for plant supplement take-up, development, and environment efficiency.

V. Suggestions for Plant People group and Vegetation Elements

1. **Rhino-Intervened Changes in Plant Species Piece**
The supplement inputs from rhino manure and the adjustments in soil piece impact plant networks inside rhino territories. Certain plant species might answer decidedly to the supplement improvement given by rhino exercises, prompting shifts in vegetation elements.

2. **Improved Plant Variety and Biodiversity Areas of interest**
The impact of rhino exercises on soil sythesis adds to upgraded plant variety, making biodiversity areas of interest inside their environments. The formation of different microenvironments through floundering and supplement cycling upholds the conjunction of an assortment of plant animal groups.

3. **Flexibility of Biological systems to Natural Pressure**

Rhino-interceded changes in soil creation add to the strength of biological systems to ecological stressors. The supplement data sources and modifications in soil structure upgrade the limit of vegetation to endure aggravations like dry spell, supporting in general biological system wellbeing.

VI. Preservation Contemplations: Adjusting Rhino Populaces and Biological system Wellbeing

1. **Populace Elements and Soil-Environment Harmony**
Preservation endeavors should think about the sensitive harmony between rhino populaces and the soundness of environments. Populace elements and natural surroundings the executives methodologies assume a urgent part in keeping up with the balance between rhino exercises and soil-environment elements.

2. **Impacts of Human-Untamed life Struggle on Soil Arrangement**
Human-natural life struggle, especially cases of territory fracture and poaching, can disturb rhino populaces and their biological jobs. This disturbance can have direct outcomes on soil arrangement and biological system wellbeing, underscoring the requirement for preservation procedures that address these difficulties.

3. **Local area Commitment in Rhino Preservation**

Connecting with nearby networks in rhino protection is fundamental to guaranteeing the supported soundness of biological systems. Local area based preservation drives that underline the environmental significance of rhinos and their dirt interceded commitments can cultivate a feeling of shared liability.

VII. Future Exploration Headings: Propelling Comprehension we might interpret Rhino-Soil Collaborations

1. **Evaluating Supplement Data sources and Cycling Rates**
   Progressions in research procedures, including isotopic examinations and sub-atomic strategies, can improve our capacity to measure supplement inputs from rhino manure and comprehend the paces of supplement cycling in soils affected by rhino exercises.
2. **Long haul Observing of Vegetation Elements**

Long haul checking of vegetation elements inside rhino natural surroundings gives bits of knowledge into the supported effect of rhino-interceded changes in soil piece. This exploration bearing adds to a more exhaustive comprehension of the environmental heritage left by rhino populaces.

4.3 Water Source Dynamics in Rhino Habitats
The Significance of Water Sources in Rhino Environments

1. **Water as a Life saver for Biological systems**
   Water is a crucial asset that supports life and shapes the construction and capability of biological systems. In rhino territories, water sources are basic for the endurance of rhinos as well as for supporting a different exhibit of natural life and adding to generally speaking environment wellbeing.
2. **Rhinos as Biological system Architects: Affecting Water Elements**

Rhinos, as megaherbivores and biological system engineers, effectively add to the elements of water sources inside their environments. Through ways of behaving like floundering and touching, rhinos impact the accessibility and dissemination of water, making one of a kind biological circumstances that echo through the environment.

II. Floundering Conduct: Making Microhabitats and Improving Water Accessibility

1. **Floundering as a Multifunctional Conduct**
   Floundering is a particular way of behaving showed by rhinos, including the making of mud dejections by blending soil in with water. While customarily connected with thermoregulation and parasite control, floundering has more extensive ramifications for water accessibility and microhabitat creation.

2. **Microhabitat Creation and Biodiversity Areas of interest**
Floundering destinations become microhabitats that have a different cluster of life. The dampness holding properties of flounders support the development of explicit plant species and draw in different organic entities, adding to biodiversity areas of interest inside rhino environments.
3. **Water Maintenance and Accessibility**

Floundering destinations act as confined water repositories. The mud in flounders holds dampness, giving a solid water source to untamed life during dry periods. This conduct grandstands the interconnected elements among rhinos and water accessibility, impacting the conveyance of life inside their natural surroundings.

III. Influence on Soil Dampness and Vegetation

1. **Soil Dampness Maintenance and Supplement Cycling**
Floundering adds to soil dampness maintenance in rhino territories. The dampness rich mud improves the fruitfulness of the dirt, affecting supplement cycling and supporting the development of vegetation. This powerful cooperation highlights the comprehensive impact of rhino conduct on both soil and water elements.
2. **Vegetation Reaction to Floundering**

The impact of floundering stretches out to vegetation elements. Certain plant species answer emphatically to the supplement rich circumstances made by floundering, prompting changes in plant arrangement and dissemination. The transaction between rhino conduct, soil dampness, and vegetation features the perplexing snare of connections inside environments.

IV. Normal Water Sources and Rhino Reliance

1. **Rhino Dependence on Regular Water Sources**
While floundering conduct adds to confined water accessibility, rhinos additionally depend on normal water sources like streams, lakes, and waterholes. The reliance of rhinos on these sources makes them central members in the more extensive water elements of their natural surroundings.
2. **Water as a Social occasion Point for Untamed life**
Regular water sources act as social event focuses for an assortment of untamed life, making centers of biological action. The presence of rhinos at waterholes impacts the way of behaving of different species and adds to the general biodiversity and biological lavishness of these areas.
3. **Water-Subordinate Vegetation Zones**

The accessibility of water impacts the dispersion of vegetation inside rhino natural surroundings. Water-subordinate vegetation zones, formed by the closeness to normal water sources, make unmistakable environmental specialties that help different plant networks and add to territory heterogeneity.

V. Protection Difficulties: Human-Natural life Struggle and Water Access

1. **Human-Untamed life Struggle over Water Access**
   As human populaces grow, the opposition for water assets escalates. Human-untamed life struggle might emerge over admittance to water, presenting difficulties for the two rhinos and nearby networks. Preservation techniques should address these struggles to guarantee the proceeded with accessibility of water for rhinos and the conjunction of untamed life and human populaces.

2. **Environment Discontinuity and Water Source Segregation**

Environment discontinuity coming about because of human exercises can prompt the segregation of water sources. The effect of divided living spaces on rhino populaces and their admittance to water highlights the requirement for protection estimates that address environment network and guarantee the free development of rhinos.

VI. Preservation Techniques: Adjusting Water Elements and Human Requirements

1. **Water The board in Safeguarded Regions**
   Successful water the board inside safeguarded regions is essential for protecting the strength of rhino living spaces. Preservation drives ought to zero in on keeping up with normal water sources, guaranteeing their availability to rhinos and other untamed life, and carrying out feasible water the board rehearses.

2. **Local area Commitment in Water Protection**
   Drawing in neighborhood networks in water preservation endeavors is fundamental for supportable conjunction. Local area based drives that advance dependable water use and underscore the natural significance of water sources add to a mutual perspective of the interconnected connections inside environments.

3. **Territory Rebuilding and Network**

Territory rebuilding projects that intend to upgrade network between divided regions can further develop admittance to water for rhinos and other natural life. These drives assume a crucial part in relieving the effects of environment fracture and supporting the normal development examples of rhinos.

VII. Future Exploration Bearings: Propelling Comprehension we might interpret Rhino-Water Elements

1. **Evaluating the Effect of Floundering on Soil and Water Science**
   Headways in research procedures, including substance examinations and iso-topic examinations, can give a more nuanced comprehension of the effect of floundering on soil and water science. This exploration heading adds to evaluating the commitments of rhino conduct to water elements.
2. **Long haul Observing of Waterhole Elements**

Long haul observing of waterhole elements, including water levels, switches in vegetation up water sources, and untamed life conduct, offers experiences into the supported effect of rhinos on water accessibility. This examination road adds to a thorough comprehension of the biological heritage left by rhino populaces.

Supporting Water Elements for Rhino Environments and Biological systems

Water sources are an indispensable part of rhino territories, impacting the ways of behaving, developments, and natural cooperations of rhinos and the more extensive biological system. From floundering conduct making microhabitats to the dependence on regular water sources, the many-sided connections among rhinos and water elements highlight the natural significance of keeping up with water accessibility.

As preservation endeavors develop to address the difficulties of human untamed life struggle and territory corruption, a comprehensive methodology that considers the fragile harmony between rhino populaces and water assets is fundamental. Through people group commitment, territory reclamation, and progressing logical exploration, we can guarantee the supported soundness of rhino natural surroundings, cultivating strong environments where rhinos and various untamed life coincide agreeably.

Chapter 5

Biodiversity Hotspots

Biodiversity areas of interest are pivotal regions on our planet that harbor an uncommon grouping of endemic species and face extreme dangers of environment obliteration. These areas of interest assume a urgent part in keeping up with the World's environmental equilibrium, giving a rich embroidery of life that upholds different biological systems and adds to the general prosperity of the planet. In this exhaustive investigation, we will dive into the idea of biodiversity areas of interest, their importance, the dangers they face, protection endeavors, and the worldwide ramifications of safeguarding these priceless locales.

1. **Figuring out Biodiversity Areas of interest:**
1. **Definition and Measures:**
   Biodiversity areas of interest are characterized by their one of a kind blend of high species wealth and high endemism. Dr. Russell Mittermeier and partners presented the idea in 1988, laying out measures for an area to be viewed as an area of interest, including at least 1,500 vascular plant species as endemics and having lost something like 70% of its unique environment.
2. **Worldwide Conveyance:**

A review of biodiversity areas of interest uncovers their worldwide dispersion, featuring locales like the Western Ghats in India, the Atlantic Timberland in Brazil, and the Mediterranean Bowl. Understanding the conveyance of areas of interest is urgent for creating compelling preservation techniques.

II. Meaning of Biodiversity Areas of interest:

1. **Environmental Significance:**
   Biodiversity areas of interest are the repositories of Earth's natural variety, giving fundamental biological system administrations like fertilization, water filtration,

and environment guideline. The many-sided trap of cooperations among species in these areas supports life and guarantees the versatility of environments.

2. **Drug and Rural Potential:**

A large number of the plant and creature species found in areas of interest have undiscovered capacity for restorative and farming applications. The rich biodiversity fills in as a wellspring of motivation for drugs and may hold the way to tackling worldwide difficulties connected with food security.

III. Dangers to Biodiversity Areas of interest:

1. **Territory Obliteration:**
   One of the main dangers to biodiversity areas of interest is territory obliteration, principally determined by human exercises like deforestation, urbanization, and farming. The deficiency of normal environments comes down on endemic species, prompting populace decline and, now and again, annihilation.

2. **Environmental Change:**
   Worldwide environmental change represents a serious danger to biodiversity areas of interest. Climbing temperatures, changed precipitation examples, and outrageous climate occasions can disturb biological systems, influencing the conveyance and endurance of species adjusted to explicit climatic circumstances.

3. **Obtrusive Species and Contamination:**

The presentation of obtrusive species and contamination further compounds the difficulties looked by biodiversity areas of interest. Intrusive species can outcompete local species, prompting populace declines, while contamination can debase environments and mischief the wellbeing of occupant species.

IV. Protection Endeavors:

1. **Safeguarded Regions and Stores:**
   Laying out safeguarded regions and stores is a major preservation methodology for protecting biodiversity areas of interest. These regions act as safe-havens where species can flourish without the quick danger of environment annihilation.

2. **Manageable Turn of events:**
   Advancing manageable advancement rehearses that offset human necessities with biological protection is fundamental for the drawn out reasonability of biodiversity areas of interest. This includes drawing in nearby networks, consolidating customary information, and carrying out harmless to the ecosystem rehearses.

3. **Global Coordinated effort:**

Biodiversity protection is a worldwide test that requires global collaboration. Cooperative endeavors among legislatures, non-administrative associations, and mainstream researchers are pivotal for tending to transboundary issues and guaranteeing the progress of preservation drives.

V. Contextual analyses:

1. **Western Ghats, India:**
   Investigate the novel biodiversity of the Western Ghats, its social importance, and the preservation endeavors in progress to shield this area of interest from dangers, for example, living space discontinuity and environmental change.
2. **Sundaland, Southeast Asia:**

Explore the biodiversity areas of interest in the Sundaland district, including the islands of Borneo and Sumatra. Dive into the difficulties presented by palm oil estates, logging, and unlawful untamed life exchange.

VI. Future Possibilities:

1. **Arising Preservation Innovations:**
   Look at the job of arising advances, for example, satellite symbolism, DNA barcoding, and computerized reasoning, in improving protection endeavors. These apparatuses can help with observing biodiversity, recognizing dangers, and executing designated preservation techniques.
2. **The Job of Native Information:**

Perceive the significance of native information in biodiversity protection. Native people group frequently have important experiences into neighborhood biological systems and can contribute fundamentally to economical preservation rehearses.

VII. Worldwide Ramifications:

1. **Biodiversity and Human Prosperity:**
   Talk about the many-sided association among biodiversity and human prosperity. The deficiency of biodiversity influences the soundness of biological systems as well as has direct ramifications for human populaces, remembering influences for farming, water assets, and sickness elements.
2. **Global Strategies and Arrangements:**

Investigate the job of global strategies and arrangements, like the Show on Natural Variety (CBD) and the Paris Understanding, in tending to biodiversity misfortune and environmental change. Investigate the victories and inadequacies of these worldwide drives.

5.1 Rhinos as Umbrella Species

Rhinos, superb animals that meander the prairies and savannas of Africa and Asia, are notable delegates of Earth's megafauna as well as serve a pivotal job as umbrella species in the domain of biodiversity protection.

This complete investigation dives into the idea of umbrella species, the meaning of rhinos in this specific situation, the difficulties they face, and the more extensive ramifications for environment wellbeing and protection.

1. **Figuring out Umbrella Species:**
1. **Definition and Idea:**
   Umbrella species are those whose preservation needs incorporate the necessities of a more extensive scope of species sharing their natural surroundings. Safeguarding umbrella species in a roundabout way shields the whole environment, as these species frequently have huge home reaches and one of a kind natural prerequisites.
2. **Job in Preservation Arranging:**

The idea of umbrella species assumes a significant part in preservation arranging, assisting with distinguishing central species whose security helps a huge number of different living beings having a similar natural surroundings. This approach is particularly important for huge, lead species like rhinos.

II. Rhinos as Umbrella Species:

1. **Species Variety in Rhino Environments:**
   Rhino environments are unbelievably different, supporting an extensive variety of verdure. The assurance of rhino living spaces intrinsically includes rationing these biological systems, which, thusly, benefits various species that share a similar climate.
2. **Enormous Home Reaches:**

Rhinos, especially the white and dark rhinoceros species, have broad home reaches. Safeguarding these huge domains guarantees the conservation of different environments and the species that occupy them.

III. Meaning of Rhinos in Biological system Wellbeing:

1. **Environmental Effect of Rhinos:**
   Rhinos are urgent for keeping up with environment wellbeing through their job as slow eaters and programs. Their taking care of propensities impact vegetation structure, seed dispersal, and supplement cycling, adding to the general equilibrium of the biological system.
2. **Biodiversity Upkeep:**

The presence of rhinos in an environment keeps up with biodiversity by forestalling the strength of specific plant species. Through their specific brushing, rhinos make a mosaic of natural surroundings that help various plant and creature life.

IV. Dangers to Rhino Populaces:

1. **Poaching for Horns:**
   Rhinos face a serious danger from poaching driven by the interest for their horns, which are erroneously accepted to have restorative properties. The unlawful natural life exchange has prompted a critical decrease in rhino populaces, especially in Africa.

2. **Living space Misfortune and Fracture:**
   Human exercises, like agribusiness, logging, and framework improvement, add to natural surroundings misfortune and discontinuity. These variables upset rhino environments, prompting secluded populaces and decreased hereditary variety.

3. **Human-Untamed life Struggle:**

As human populaces grow, clashes among rhinos and neighborhood networks emerge. Crop striking and occurrences of human-natural life struggle present difficulties to rhino preservation endeavors and require practical arrangements that benefit the two people and natural life.

V. Preservation Drives:

1. **Safeguarded Regions and Stores:**
   Laying out and keeping up with safeguarded regions and stores is a central procedure for rhino protection. These regions give a place of refuge to rhinos and different species, advancing biodiversity preservation.

2. **Hostile to Poaching Measures:**
   Endeavors to battle poaching incorporate the organization of hostile to poaching watches, the utilization of innovation like robots and GPS beacons, and worldwide coordinated efforts to address the interest for rhino horns.

3. **Local area Contribution and Practical Turn of events:**

Including neighborhood networks in protection endeavors is fundamental. Practical improvement drives that consider the necessities of the two individuals and untamed life assist with alleviating human-untamed life clashes and accumulate support for rhino preservation.

VI. Examples of overcoming adversity:

1. **South Africa's Endeavors:**
   Investigate South Africa's triumphs in rhino protection, including the execution

of hostile to poaching measures, local area contribution, and creative methodologies, for example, dehorning to discourage poachers.

2. **Indian Rhino Preservation:**

Feature the preservation outcome of Indian rhinoceros populaces, especially in Kaziranga Public Park, displaying the positive effect of devoted protection endeavors.

VII. Worldwide Ramifications:

1. **Rhinos and Worldwide Biodiversity:**
   Analyze the more extensive ramifications of rhino protection on worldwide biodiversity. The conservation of rhino territories and populaces adds to the upkeep of solid environments with benefits arriving at a long ways past their nearby environmental factors.
2. **Examples for Preservation Techniques:**

Ponder the illustrations gained from rhino protection endeavors and their pertinence to the more extensive field of preservation. The difficulties looked by rhinos equal those of numerous different species, making their preservation procedures significant on a worldwide scale.

VIII. Future Viewpoints:

1. **Arising Advances in Preservation:**
   Investigate the job of arising advances, like DNA examination, satellite following, and man-made consciousness, in improving rhino protection endeavors. These devices can support observing populaces, distinguishing dangers, and executing designated protection measures.
2. **Environmental Change and Natural surroundings Variation:**

Consider the effect of environmental change on rhino natural surroundings and the requirement for versatile preservation techniques. Environment tough protection plans can assist with guaranteeing the drawn out practicality of rhino populaces in an evolving climate.

5.2 Protection of Biodiversity in Rhino-Inhabited Areas

Biodiversity protection in regions occupied by rhinos is a perplexing and multi-layered challenge that requests extensive systems to guarantee the endurance of these famous species as well as the bunch of widely varied vegetation that share their territories. This broad investigation digs into the complexities of safeguarding biodiversity in rhino-occupied regions, tending to the natural meaning of these locales, the dangers they face, and the assorted protection endeavors executed to get the fate of the two rhinos and the biological systems they occupy.

1. **Natural Meaning of Rhino-Possessed Regions:**
1. **Biodiversity Areas of interest:**
   Rhino-occupied regions frequently concur with biodiversity areas of interest, districts described by high species lavishness and endemism. These regions are significant repositories of biodiversity, supporting a large number of plant and creature species that add to the general strength of biological systems.
2. **Cornerstone Species:**

Rhinos assume an essential part as cornerstone species in their territories. Their taking care of propensities, especially the particular touching and perusing ways of behaving, impact vegetation structure, seed dispersal, and supplement cycling, molding the scene and making conditions reasonable for different species.

II. Dangers to Biodiversity in Rhino-Occupied Regions:

1. **Poaching for Rhino Horns:**
   Unlawful poaching for rhino horns stays one of the main dangers to biodiversity in rhino-occupied regions. The interest for rhino horns, driven by customary medication convictions and underground market exchange, seriously endangers rhino populaces as well as adds to the destabilization of whole environments.
2. **Natural surroundings Misfortune and Discontinuity:**
   Human exercises, including horticulture, logging, and framework advancement, lead to environment misfortune and discontinuity. The infringement of human settlements into rhino natural surroundings disturbs environments, undermining the endurance of various plant and creature species.
3. **Environmental Change Effects:**
   The impacts of environmental change, for example, adjusted precipitation examples and temperature increments, represent extra difficulties to biodiversity in rhino-occupied regions. Species adjusted to explicit climatic circumstances might confront challenges in changing, prompting shifts in dissemination and expected decreases in populaces.
4. **Human-Untamed life Struggle:**

As human populaces grow, clashes among rhinos and nearby networks become more pervasive. Crop striking and occurrences of human-natural life struggle present difficulties to both human jobs and biodiversity preservation endeavors.

III. Protection Procedures in Rhino-Occupied Regions:

1. **Safeguarded Regions and Stores:**
   Laying out and keeping up with safeguarded regions and stores is an essential procedure for the preservation of biodiversity in rhino-occupied districts. These

assigned regions give a safe-haven to rhinos and different species, guaranteeing the conservation of urgent living spaces.

2. **Hostile to Poaching Measures:**
   Endeavors to battle poaching include the organization of hostile to poaching watches, the utilization of innovation like robots and GPS beacons, and world-wide coordinated efforts to address the interest for rhino horns. Hostile to poaching measures are fundamental for safeguarding rhinos as well as the more extensive biodiversity inside their natural surroundings.

3. **Natural surroundings Rebuilding and The board:**
   Executing natural surroundings reclamation and the board programs is essential for alleviating the effects of territory misfortune and fracture. These projects expect to reestablish corrupted environments, make natural life passageways, and advance economical land-use rehearses that benefit the two people and untamed life.

4. **Local area Contribution and Economical Turn of events:**

Including neighborhood networks in preservation endeavors is critical to making long haul progress. Maintainable improvement drives that consider the necessities of the two individuals and natural life assist with moderating human-natural life clashes and accumulate support for biodiversity preservation.

IV. Contextual analyses:

1. **Kruger Public Park, South Africa:**
   Investigate the protection endeavors in Kruger Public Park, a famous hold that is home to a critical populace of rhinos. Examine the systems utilized to safeguard rhinos and the more extensive biodiversity inside the recreation area.

2. **Kaziranga Public Park, India:**

Analyze the preservation outcome of Kaziranga Public Park, especially in safeguarding the Indian rhinoceros. Feature the incorporated methodology that tends to poaching, environment the board, and local area inclusion.

V. Mechanical Advancements in Biodiversity Preservation:

1. **Reconnaissance and Checking Advancements:**
   Examine the job of cutting edge innovations, for example, satellite symbolism, camera traps, and acoustic observing, in reconnaissance and checking endeavors. These innovations upgrade our capacity to follow rhino populaces, identify poaching exercises, and accumulate important information on biodiversity.

2. **Hereditary and Conceptive Advancements:**

Investigate hereditary and conceptive advancements, remembering for vitro treatment and hereditary profiling, as apparatuses for upgrading rhino preservation endeavors. These advances can add to keeping up with hereditary variety and tending to difficulties, for example, low rhino rates of birth.

VI. Worldwide Joint effort and Strategy Drives:

1. **Peaceful accords and Settlements:**
   Analyze the job of peaceful accords and arrangements, for example, the Show on Worldwide Exchange Jeopardized Types of Wild Fauna and Verdure (Refers to) and the Show on Organic Variety (CBD), in molding worldwide endeavors to safeguard rhinos and biodiversity.

2. **Transboundary Protection Drives:**

Feature the significance of transboundary preservation drives that include joint effort between nations to safeguard shared rhino populaces and their natural surroundings. These drives are urgent for tending to difficulties that stretch out past public boundaries.

VII. Difficulties and Future Contemplations:

1. **Arising Dangers:**
   Consider arising dangers to biodiversity in rhino-possessed regions, like new illnesses, obtrusive species, and the advancing effects of environmental change. Expecting and tending to these difficulties is fundamental for versatile protection procedures.

2. **Financial Elements:**

Look at the financial elements that impact preservation endeavors. Adjusting the necessities of nearby networks with the basic to safeguard biodiversity requires resolving issues of destitution, training, and elective occupations.

VIII. Future Points of view:

1. **Maintainable The travel industry and Protection Funding:**
   Investigate the capability of maintainable the travel industry as a wellspring of financing for biodiversity preservation. Mindful the travel industry practices can add to nearby economies and backing preservation drives in rhino-occupied regions.

2. **Training and Mindfulness:**

Feature the significance of training and mindfulness programs in encouraging a preservation disapproved of society. Teaching nearby networks, policymakers, and the overall population is significant for gathering backing and cultivating a feeling of obligation toward biodiversity.

5.3 Conservation Strategies to Safeguard Ecosystem Diversity

Monitoring biological system variety is a complex test that requests exhaustive procedures to defend the unpredictable equilibrium of life on The planet. As anthropogenic exercises keep on presenting dangers to environments around the world, the requirement for compelling protection measures turns out to be progressively critical. This investigation digs into the key preservation methodologies utilized to shield biological system variety, tending to the environmental meaning of assorted environments, the dangers they face, and the different methodologies carried out to guarantee their drawn out wellbeing and flexibility.

1. **Biological Meaning of Environment Variety:**

   Environment variety, enveloping various territories and biotic networks, assumes a basic part in keeping up with the planet's natural equilibrium. Various environments give a heap of administrations, including supplement cycling, fertilization, water sanitization, and environment guideline. The many-sided trap of communications among species inside assorted biological systems adds to their strength and capacity to adjust to natural changes.

2. **Dangers to Biological system Variety:**

   In spite of their significance, environments face a variety of dangers, basically determined by human exercises. Territory annihilation, contamination, environmental change, and the presentation of obtrusive species are among the key elements adding to the corruption of biological systems. Understanding these dangers is vital for creating designated preservation systems.

3. **Safeguarded Regions and Biodiversity Stores:**

   One of the foundation systems in preserving environment variety is the foundation and viable administration of safeguarded regions and biodiversity saves. These regions go about as safe-havens where regular cycles can happen without the quick danger of human impedance. They act as critical environments for many species, adding to generally biodiversity protection.

4. **Natural surroundings Reclamation and Restoration:**

   Perceiving the effects of natural surroundings misfortune, preservation endeavors progressively stress living space reclamation and restoration. Rebuilding projects intend to renew debased environments by once again introducing local vegetation, controlling intrusive species, and carrying out maintainable land-use rehearses. The rebuilding of living spaces upgrades their ability to help different greenery.

5. **Feasible Asset The executives:**

   Advancing economical asset the executives rehearses is fundamental for moderating biological system variety. Overexploitation of regular assets, like deforestation, overfishing, and inordinate hunting, can prompt the exhaustion of species and disturb environment elements. Supportable practices guarantee the proceeded with accessibility of assets while limiting adverse consequences on biodiversity.

6. **Environmental Change Alleviation and Transformation:**
As environmental change represents a developing danger to biological systems, preservation procedures should integrate relief and variation measures. Alleviation endeavors mean to lessen ozone depleting substance discharges, while variation methodologies center around assisting biological systems with adapting to the evolving environment. This might include making movement halls, safeguarding weak species, and improving generally speaking biological system versatility.

7. **Local area Based Protection:**
Including neighborhood networks in preservation endeavors is fundamental to the outcome of biodiversity assurance. Local area based protection methodologies perceive the interconnectedness between human prosperity and biological system wellbeing. Drawing in neighborhood networks in dynamic cycles, giving elective occupations, and cultivating ecological schooling add to economical protection rehearses.

8. **Availability Preservation:**
Keeping up with environmental network is essential for saving biological system variety, particularly in divided scenes. Network protection includes making untamed life halls and guaranteeing unrestricted pathways for species development. This works with quality stream, forestalls confinement of populaces, and supports biological system capabilities across bigger scenes.

9. **Logical Exploration and Observing:**
Logical examination and observing assume a critical part in preservation procedures. Understanding the biological elements of environments, following populace drifts, and evaluating the effects of different stressors give the establishment to prove based protection drives. Cutting edge innovations, for example, remote detecting and DNA investigation, improve our capacity to assemble exact information for informed navigation.

10. **Worldwide Coordinated effort and Strategy Drives:**
Preserving biological system variety requires worldwide participation and strategy structures. Peaceful accords, like the Show on Natural Variety (CBD), set up for composed endeavors to address biodiversity misfortune. Cooperative drives including legislatures, non-legislative associations, and mainstream researchers add to a brought together way to deal with protection on a worldwide scale.

11. **Training and Effort Projects:**
Bringing issues to light and encouraging a feeling of ecological stewardship are indispensable parts of protection methodologies. Instruction and effort

programs designated at schools, networks, and the overall population advance a more profound comprehension of the worth of biodiversity. Educated and drawn in people are bound to help protection drives and promoter for economical practices.

12. **Preservation Hereditary qualities and Biotechnology:**
Preservation hereditary qualities and biotechnology assume arising parts in protecting environment variety. Hereditary methods, like hostage reproducing and hereditary salvage, can assist with reestablishing populaces confronting hereditary decay. Biotechnological devices, including quality altering, hold potential for tending to explicit dangers and upgrading the versatility of weak species.

13. **Challenges and Moral Contemplations:**
While preservation methodologies expect to safeguard environment variety, they are not without challenges and moral contemplations. Adjusting the necessities of human populaces with preservation objectives, tending to clashes among partners, and exploring moral contemplations connected with mediations in regular cycles are progressing difficulties in the field.

14. **Contextual investigations:**
1. **Yellowstone Public Park, USA:**
Investigate the fruitful preservation endeavors in Yellowstone Public Park, featuring the rebuilding of wolf populaces and the flowing impacts on the whole biological system. This contextual analysis shows the interconnectedness of species and the significance of cornerstone species in keeping up with environment variety.
2. **Extraordinary Hindrance Reef, Australia:**

Analyze the preservation challenges confronting the Incomparable Boundary Reef, one of the world's most assorted marine biological systems. Break down the endeavors to alleviate coral blanching, control obtrusive species, and address the more extensive effects of environmental change on this notorious reef framework.

XV. Future Points of view:

1. **Arising Advances and Developments:**
Think about the likely effect of arising innovations, like computerized reasoning, drones, and high level checking frameworks, on the fate of protection. These advancements might alter our capacity to screen biological systems, answer dangers, and carry out designated protection techniques.
2. **Coordination of Native Information:**

Perceive the benefit of incorporating native information into preservation rehearses. Native people group frequently have conventional biological information that can supplement logical comprehension and add to all encompassing protection moves toward that regard social variety.

Chapter 6

Downstream Effects on Water Ecosystems

Downstream consequences for water environments allude to the effect of different exercises, contaminations, and changes happening upstream on the quality and soundness of water bodies farther downstream. These impacts are essential to comprehend as they assume a huge part in molding the by and large biological equilibrium and maintainability of oceanic conditions. This exhaustive investigation will dig into the different parts of downstream impacts on water environments, enveloping both regular and anthropogenic impacts.

1. **Hydrological Changes:**
   The primary downstream impact includes adjustments in the hydrological attributes of water bodies. Dams, water system, and urbanization upstream can change the stream designs, silt transport, and water temperature downstream. These progressions can upset the normal equilibrium of oceanic environments, influencing the natural surroundings of different species and affecting their regenerative cycles.
2. **Sedimentation and Natural surroundings Modifications:**
   One of the most articulated downstream impacts is sedimentation. Soil disintegration from deforested regions, farming overflow, or development exercises upstream can prompt an expanded dregs load in downstream waters. This overabundance sedimentation can adversely influence amphibian natural surroundings by covering the riverbed, diminishing light infiltration, and changing the construction of submerged environments.
3. **Water Quality and Contamination:**
   Poisons delivered into water bodies upstream can have expansive results on downstream biological systems. Modern releases, horticultural spillover containing pesticides and composts, and untreated sewage all add to water contamination. As these poisons travel downstream, they can gather, prompting a decrease

in water quality, influencing sea-going organic entities, and presenting dangers to human wellbeing in downstream networks dependent on these water sources.

4. **Biodiversity and Species Cooperations:**
Downstream impacts significantly affect biodiversity and the perplexing trap of species associations inside amphibian environments. Changes in water temperature, territory construction, and supplement accessibility can lean toward specific species while disadvantaging others. This can prompt changes in the piece of sea-going networks, influencing the overflow and dispersion of species downstream.

5. **Stream System Changes:**
Human exercises, for example, dam development and water extraction upstream can essentially modify the normal stream systems of streams. These changes can affect the timing and term of floods and dry spells downstream, impacting the biological cycles fundamental for the endurance and generation of sea-going creatures. For instance, the modification of stream systems can disturb fish relocation designs and impede the dispersal of oceanic plants.

6. **Supplement Elements and Eutrophication:**
Supplement inputs from agribusiness, sewage, and modern releases upstream can cause eutrophication downstream. Exorbitant supplements, especially nitrogen and phosphorus, can prompt the excess of green growth and oceanic plants. This can bring about oxygen exhaustion in the water, hurting fish and different creatures subject to all around oxygenated conditions. Downstream regions might encounter algal blossoms, making no man's lands impeding to amphibian life.

7. **Influence on Riparian Zones:**
Downstream impacts reach out past the amphibian climate to affect riparian zones — regions along the banks of waterways and streams. Changes in water stream, sedimentation, and supplement levels can impact the construction and sythesis of vegetation in these zones. This, thus, influences the living space quality for both amphibian and earthbound creatures, affecting the general biodiversity of the environment.

8. **Environmental Change and Downstream Impacts:**
The approaching apparition of environmental change compounds downstream impacts on water biological systems. Modified precipitation designs, climbing temperatures, and changes in climate limits can enhance the difficulties looked by downstream conditions. These effects might incorporate more continuous and serious floods, delayed dry spells, and changed occasional examples, all of which have flowing impacts on the wellbeing and versatility of amphibian environments.

9. **Human Effects and Cultural Worries:**
Downstream impacts are not restricted to environmental results alone; they

likewise have critical cultural ramifications. Networks depending on downstream water hotspots for drinking, farming, and amusement might confront difficulties connected with water quality, accessibility, and the deficiency of environment administrations. Understanding these downstream effects is urgent for compelling water asset the executives and maintainable turn of events.

10. **Alleviation Procedures and Rebuilding Endeavors:**
Perceiving the significance of alleviating downstream impacts, different procedures and rebuilding endeavors have been utilized. These may remember the execution of best administration rehearses for agribusiness, the development of dregs bowls to lessen soil disintegration, and the advancement of water treatment innovations. Moreover, the decommissioning of out of date dams and the rebuilding of regular stream systems are fundamental stages in protecting downstream environments.

11. **Incorporated Watershed The board:**
A viable way to deal with address downstream impacts includes taking on incorporated watershed the executives rehearses. This all encompassing procedure thinks about the whole watershed, including both upstream and downstream regions, perceiving the interconnectedness of biological systems. By consolidating land-use arranging, reasonable ranger service, and mindful metropolitan turn of events, incorporated watershed the board expects to offset human requirements with biological supportability.

12. **Research Holes and Future Headings:**

In spite of critical progressions in seeing downstream consequences for water biological systems, there remain holes in information that warrant further examination. Long haul checking studies, combined with interdisciplinary exploration draws near, can upgrade how we might interpret complex biological cycles. Future examination ought to likewise investigate the combined and synergistic effects of different stressors on downstream biological systems to foster more far reaching alleviation and reclamation procedures.

6.1 Rhino Influence on Water Quality and Availability

Rhinos, charming megafauna fundamentally connected with earthly environments, impact the quality and accessibility of water in their living spaces. This exposition investigates the different manners by which rhinos influence water assets, from their searching propensities to their part in molding scene elements. Understanding the complicated connection among rhinos and water quality is critical not just for the protection of these famous species yet additionally for economical water asset the board.

II. Rhino Nature and Conduct

Rhinos, containing species like the white rhinoceros (Ceratotherium simum) and dark rhinoceros (Diceros bicornis), assume a fundamental part in biological systems because of their exceptional natural qualities. These incorporate their natural surroundings inclinations, appropriation, and unmistakable taking care of propensities. Understanding the environment and conduct of rhinos is central to appreciating their impact on water quality and accessibility.

III. Scene Designing by Rhinos

One of the key ways rhinos influence water assets is through their job as scene engineers. The monstrous size and weight of rhinos add to soil compaction as they travel through their living spaces. This part investigates what soil compaction means for water penetration and spillover, stressing the positive and negative parts of this interaction.

IV. Formation of Water Openings

Rhinos add to the creation and upkeep of water openings through their floundering conduct. This segment looks at the meaning of these water openings as critical watering focuses for different natural life. It dives into the occasional varieties in water accessibility and the significance of rhino exercises in guaranteeing admittance to water, particularly during dry periods.

V. Impact on Plant People group

Rhinos' particular herbivory impacts the piece and design of plant networks in their living spaces. This part investigates the flowing consequences for supplement cycling, water use proficiency, and water accessibility coming about because of rhinos' inclinations for specific plant species. It stresses the environmental ramifications of these effects on generally speaking water quality.

VI. Supplement Cycling and Water Quality

The testimony of rhino excrement and pee adds to supplement cycling in environments. This segment researches the positive and negative parts of supplement cycling by rhinos, talking about the effects on soil richness, vegetation wellbeing, and potential water quality issues like eutrophication.

VII. Influence on Stream Bank Dependability

Rhinos' development along stream banks can impact bank dependability, influencing disintegration and sedimentation processes. This part investigates the connections among rhinos and transfer biological systems, featuring the expected ramifications for water quality downstream and the more extensive oceanic climate.

VIII. Job in Wetland Biological systems

Wetlands are especially delicate to changes in water elements, and rhinos, as occupants of these region, assume a fundamental part. This segment explores how rhinos shape wetland biological systems, impacting water levels, vegetation design, and supplement cycling. It investigates the interconnectedness of rhinos with wetland conditions and their commitments to water quality in these significant environments.

IX. Protection Difficulties and Water Assets

Regardless of their positive commitments, rhinos face extreme preservation difficulties like poaching and living space misfortune. This segment talks about the ramifications of these moves on the capacity of rhinos to keep impacting water assets emphatically. It stresses the significance of protection endeavors for rhino populaces as well as for keeping up with biological cycles connected with water quality and accessibility.

X. Environmental Change and Variation

The effect of environmental change acquaints extra intricacies with the connection among rhinos and water assets. This segment investigates how changes in precipitation examples, temperature, and outrageous climate occasions might impact the accessibility of water in rhino natural surroundings. It examines the versatile procedures of rhinos and the more extensive natural ramifications for water quality and accessibility notwithstanding environment related difficulties.

XI. Local area Inclusion and Maintainable Practices

In districts where rhinos coincide with human networks, feasible practices become vital. This part examines the significance of local area association in rhino protection and the advancement of reasonable land-use rehearses. It investigates how adjusting the necessities of the two people and untamed life adds to the drawn out strength of rhino living spaces and the related water assets.

XII. Research Holes and Future Bearings

While the ebb and flow comprehension of the connection among rhinos and water assets is developing, there are still examination holes that warrant further investigation. This segment examines the requirement for long haul observing investigations, inter-disciplinary examination draws near, and the investigation of total and synergistic effects. It accentuates the significance of progressing examination to upgrade how we might interpret the complex environmental cycles associated with rhino effect on water quality and accessibility.

6.2 Impact on Fish and Amphibian Populations

Fish and creatures of land and water, as key parts of amphibian biological systems, assume critical parts in keeping up with natural equilibrium. Nonetheless, human exercises have progressively upset these sensitive biological systems, presenting serious dangers to the populaces of fish and creatures of land and water. This exposition will dig into the multi-layered effects of human activities, going from territory obliteration to environmental change, on these crucial species.

II. Living space Obliteration and Change

1. **Deforestation and Urbanization:**

   Deforestation and urbanization are huge supporters of territory annihilation, influencing fish and land and water proficient populaces. The getting free from woods for farming and metropolitan advancement prompts the deficiency of basic territories for these species. Decreased vegetation along water bodies, an outcome of deforestation and metropolitan extension, increments sedimentation, adversely influencing fish generating grounds and land and water proficient rearing locales.

2. **Contamination:**
   Contamination, coming about because of modern and rural overflow, represents an immediate danger to fish and creatures of land and water. Synthetic compounds, pesticides, and weighty metals find their direction into water bodies, modifying water quality. This contamination disturbs the wellbeing of fish, slows down their regenerative cycles, and can be deadly to creatures of land and water at different phases of their life cycle.

3. **Dams and Hydroelectric Tasks:**

The development of dams and hydroelectric tasks has significant outcomes on amphibian environments. Modifications to regular waterway stream influence fish movement designs, thwarting their capacity to reach bringing forth grounds. The discontinuity of living spaces brought about by dam development separates populaces, decreasing hereditary variety and expanding the weakness of fish and creatures of land and water to natural changes.

III. Environmental Change Effects

1. **Temperature Changes:**
   Climbing temperatures related with environmental change straightforwardly influence fish and creatures of land and water. Fish, being ectothermic, are profoundly delicate to temperature changes. Changes in temperature impact fish digestion, development rates, and conduct.
   Creatures of land and water, which frequently depend on unambiguous temperature conditions for reproducing and hibernation, may confront moves in adjusting to modified warm systems.

2. **Changed Precipitation Examples:**

Environmental change adds to shifts in precipitation designs, affecting water levels and stream. These progressions impact fish bringing forth territories and land and water proficient reproducing locales. Expanded recurrence and power of outrageous climate occasions, for example, floods or dry seasons, present direct dangers to the endurance of fish and land and water proficient populaces.

IV. Overfishing and Abuse

1. **Business and Sporting Fishing:**
   Overfishing is a worldwide worry with sweeping ramifications for fish populaces and whole biological systems. Business and sporting fishing rehearses frequently target explicit species, prompting the consumption of these populaces. The

unevenness brought about by overfishing upsets the mind boggling food web connections, influencing the two hunters and prey.

2. **Pet Exchange and Assortment:**

The pet exchange, especially for fascinating species, represents a danger to land and water proficient populaces. Creatures of land and water are frequently gathered for the pet exchange, and over-assortment can prompt decreases in their populaces. This effects the species being gathered as well as upsets the environmental jobs they play inside their natural surroundings.

V. Presentation of Obtrusive Species

1. **Influence on Local Fish:**
   The presentation of obtrusive fish species can have extreme ramifications for local populaces. Intrusive species frequently outcompete local fish for assets, disturbing the equilibrium inside biological systems. Some obtrusive fish species may likewise be hunters, representing an immediate danger to local fish populaces.

2. **Land and water proficient Chytrid Parasite:**

The presentation of the chytrid parasite is a worldwide worry for land and water proficient populaces. This microorganism, frequently spread through the global exchange of creatures of land and water, causes chytridiomycosis, an illness liable for far and wide decays and terminations. Creatures of land and water, lacking regular protections against this organism, face extreme dangers to their endurance.

VI. Protection and Relief Methodologies

1. **Living space Rebuilding:**
   Endeavors to reestablish debased natural surroundings are critical for the preservation of fish and land and water proficient populaces. Territory rebuilding projects include replanting vegetation, eliminating intrusive species, and alleviating the effects of urbanization to make better environments for these species to flourish.

2. **Contamination Control Measures:**
   Carrying out contamination control measures is fundamental to safeguard water quality. Guideline and requirement of approaches that limit modern and rural spillover, as well as the appropriate treatment of wastewater, are basic moves toward lessening contamination and its unfavorable impacts on fish and creatures of land and water.

3. **Environmental Change Relief:**
   Addressing environmental change requires worldwide endeavors to lessen ozone depleting substance outflows. Drives zeroed in on progressing to environmentally

friendly power sources, reasonable land-use practices, and approaches that advance environment flexibility are essential for protecting fish and land and water proficient natural surroundings.

4. **Supportable Fishing Practices:**
Taking on economical fishing rehearses is basic for the protection of fish populaces. Carrying out get limits, keeping away from disastrous fishing strategies, and advancing mindful fishing rehearses add to keeping up with solid fish stocks and protecting biodiversity.

5. **Obtrusive Species The executives:**

Effective administration systems for intrusive species include early identification, anticipation, and control measures. These may incorporate the expulsion of obtrusive species, checking shipping lanes to forestall the presentation of new intrusive species, and public mindfulness missions to put the arrival of colorful pets into the wild down.

6.3 Linkages Between Rhino Habitats and Aquatic Ecosystems

Rhinos, notable megafauna that meander the scenes of different mainlands, are regularly connected with earthly conditions. Notwithstanding, the interconnections between rhino environments and sea-going biological systems are unpredictable and imperative. This article intends to unwind the unique linkages between the living spaces where rhinos flourish and the wellbeing of adjacent sea-going conditions. Perceiving and understanding these linkages are fundamental for all encompassing protection endeavors and reasonable administration of biological systems.

II. Rhino Living spaces: An Outline

Rhinos occupy different scenes across Africa and Asia, with different species showing one of a kind inclinations for explicit conditions. The white rhinoceros (Ceratotherium simum) and dark rhinoceros (Diceros bicornis), for example, are tracked down in savannas and meadows, while the Indian rhinoceros (Rhinoceros unicornis) favors wetlands and damp regions.

In these territories, rhinos assume a urgent part in keeping up with environment balance. Their scavenging and brushing exercises shape the construction and piece of vegetation, impacting the accessibility of assets for a bunch of animal categories. The presence of water sources inside rhino environments is a vital element for their endurance, yet it likewise makes way for interesting collaborations with neighboring oceanic biological systems.

III. Rhinos as Scene Designers

Rhinos are strong scene engineers, chiseling their environments through their particular scavenging and brushing propensities. As herbivores, rhinos assume a critical part in forming the design and elements of vegetation. Their particular taking care of ways of behaving add to the upkeep of open meadows, forestalling the infringement of woody vegetation. This, thusly, impacts the scene's hydrology and supplement cycling.

The course of particular rummaging includes rhinos consuming explicit plant species, prompting changes in the overflow and dissemination of vegetation. This particular strain can make mosaic scenes with patches of differing vegetation thickness. These patches, wealthy in biodiversity, are pivotal for rhinos as well as give natural surroundings to a huge number of different species, shaping the many-sided embroidery of earthly environments.

As rhinos travel through their territories looking for food and water, they accidentally upset the dirt. Their gigantic size and weight bring about soil compaction, making channels and despondencies that impact water stream and penetration. These modifications to the scene have direct ramifications for adjoining oceanic biological systems.

IV. Effect on Water Stream and Penetration

Rhinos' incidental scene designing quite affects water elements inside their living spaces. The compacted soil makes channels that work with water stream, possibly impacting close by streams and streams. The changed geology improves water invasion, permitting water to really penetrate the dirt more.

This upgraded penetration benefits groundwater re-energize, adding to the manageability of springs and keeping up with water accessibility in the scene. The interconnectedness between rhino environments and nearby sea-going biological systems is exemplified in the progression of water.

Precipitation that grounds on rhino-impacted scenes turns out to be essential for a hydrological network, influencing downstream water quality and accessibility.

V. Production of Water Openings

One of the most intriguing linkages between rhino natural surroundings and amphibian biological systems is the making of water openings. Rhinos take part in a way of behaving known as floundering, where they roll in mud and water to chill off and safeguard their skin from parasites. This cycle frequently prompts the arrangement of sorrows that can develop into little water openings.

These water openings act as fundamental watering focuses for a bunch of animal groups, including other huge herbivores, birds, and more modest warm blooded creatures. During dry seasons or times of dry spell, when water sources might be scant, these misleadingly made water openings become desert springs in the scene. The interconnectedness among rhinos and oceanic biological systems becomes obvious as the water openings add to the generally hydrological elements of the locale.

VI. Supplement Cycling and Water Quality

Rhinos, through their taking care of and discharge processes, essentially impact supplement cycling inside their territories. As they consume vegetation, they store supplement rich defecation in the scene. The testimony of these supplements, including nitrogen and phosphorus, adds to the richness of the dirt.

The complex association between supplement cycling and water quality becomes obvious while thinking about the downstream impacts. Precipitation washes these supplements into water bodies, affecting the supplement creation of waterways and streams neighboring rhino living spaces. While moderate supplement data sources can improve sea-going efficiency, extreme supplement spillover can prompt water quality issues, like eutrophication, with suggestions for fish and other amphibian creatures.

VII. Influence on Riparian Zones

Rhino living spaces are much of the time arranged along the banks of waterways and streams, known as riparian zones. These zones are urgent progress regions among earthly and amphibian environments, described by exceptional vegetation and different fauna. Rhinos, through their development and touching exercises, impact the construction and arrangement of riparian vegetation.

Changes in riparian vegetation can have flowing impacts on water quality and territory appropriateness for amphibian creatures. Keeping up with the trustworthiness of riparian zones is indispensable for saving water quality, forestalling disintegration, and supporting the assorted cluster of species that rely upon these temporary living spaces.

VIII. Protection Suggestions

Understanding the linkages between rhino territories and amphibian biological systems holds significant ramifications for preservation techniques. The protection of rhino populaces goes past the conservation of a solitary animal groups; it includes the whole snare of life associated with these heavenly animals.

Monitoring rhino environments includes safeguarding the earthly scenes they meander as well as the contiguous water bodies and riparian zones. Coordinated watershed the board draws near, which consider the interconnectedness of earthly and sea-going biological systems, become fundamental for supporting the wellbeing and usefulness of these conditions.

IX. Difficulties and Future Contemplations

In spite of the many-sided linkages between rhino living spaces and amphibian biological systems, various difficulties undermine their maintainability. Living space misfortune, driven by human exercises, for example, horticulture and urbanization, represents a huge danger to the two rhinos and the environments they possess. Environmental change further worsens these difficulties, with erratic precipitation examples and climbing temperatures influencing water accessibility and living space reasonableness.

Future protection endeavors should think about these difficulties and integrate versatile systems. This incorporates environment reclamation drives, environment strong land-use arranging, and measures to relieve human-natural life clashes. Also, proceeded with examination into the particular elements of the linkages between rhino living spaces and oceanic biological systems is urgent for creating informed preservation methodologies.

Chapter 7

Human-Wildlife Conflict and Conservation

Human-natural life struggle (HWC) is a complex and progressively common issue that emerges when the interests of people and natural life impact, frequently prompting unfavorable ramifications for both. As human populaces extend and normal environments shrivel, experiences among people and untamed life become more continuous, bringing about clashes that compromise the endurance of various species. This paper dives into the complex idea of human-natural life struggle, investigating its causes, influences, and the preservation procedures that intend to relieve these contentions while advancing conjunction among people and natural life.

II. Reasons for Human-Untamed life Struggle

1. **Natural surroundings Fracture:**
   The infringement of human settlements into normal territories, frequently determined by horticulture, urbanization, and foundation improvement, prompts territory fracture. As normal territories recoil and become segregated, natural life is constrained into more modest regions, improving the probability of human-natural life experiences.

2. **Contest for Assets:**
   Untamed life frequently contends with people for restricted assets like water, food, and space. Horticulture, specifically, is a typical point of convergence for clashes, as animals might strike crops looking for food, prompting monetary misfortunes for ranchers and retaliatory measures against untamed life.

3. **Environmental Change:**
   The effects of environmental change, including modified precipitation examples and natural surroundings shifts, can worsen human-untamed life clashes. Changes in asset accessibility and dispersion might drive untamed life to look for food in regions possessed by people, strengthening rivalry and struggle.

4. **Unlawful Untamed life Exchange:**

The unlawful exchange of untamed life and untamed life items can drive clashes also. Poaching and dealing exercises jeopardize species as well as elevate strains between preservationists, policing, neighborhood networks.

III. Effects of Human-Untamed life Struggle

1. **Monetary Misfortunes:**
   Ranchers and networks frequently endure the worst part of human-untamed life clashes. Crop strikes by elephants, plunder of animals by hunters, and different types of natural life harm bring about significant financial misfortunes, affecting vocations and compounding neediness in impacted regions.

2. **Domesticated animals Ravaging:**
   Predation on homegrown domesticated animals by enormous carnivores, like lions, wolves, and bears, is a typical trigger for clashes. This prompts monetary misfortunes for ranchers as well as adds to negative view of natural life, filling retaliatory killings.

3. **Loss of Living souls:**
   In outrageous cases, human-untamed life clashes can bring about fatalities on the two sides. Assaults by huge hunters or elephants can represent an immediate danger to living souls, prompting dread and hatred inside nearby networks.

4. **Mental Effect:**

Living in consistent feeling of dread toward untamed life and the monetary vulnerability related with potential contentions can meaningfully affect nearby networks. Tension, stress, and a reduced feeling of prosperity are normal results of drawn out openness to human-untamed life clashes.

IV. Protection Techniques for Alleviating Human-Natural life Struggle

1. **Local area Based Protection:**
   Connecting with neighborhood networks in preservation endeavors is vital for moderating human-natural life clashes. At the point when networks are engaged with dynamic cycles and advantage straightforwardly from preservation drives, there is a more noteworthy probability of encouraging conjunction. This might include income sharing systems, business open doors, or the advancement of local area based the travel industry.

2. **Schooling and Mindfulness:**
   Bringing issues to light about the significance of untamed life preservation and the natural jobs of various species is fundamental for cultivating understanding and resistance. Instruction projects can assist with dispersing misguided judgments about untamed life, adding to additional uplifting outlooks and diminished struggle.

3. **Elective Livelihoods:**

Giving people group elective job choices can decrease their reliance on regular assets that might draw in untamed life clashes. Feasible horticulture rehearses, eco-accommodating the travel industry, and the advancement of elective pay sources can add to both protection objectives and the prosperity of neighborhood networks.

4. **Early Admonition Frameworks and Innovation:**

The turn of events and execution of early advance notice frameworks can help networks expect and plan for possible struggles. Advancements, for example, sensor-based alerts, drone observation, and GPS following can give constant data on natural life development, taking into consideration convenient intercession and struggle anticipation.

5. **Domesticated animals Insurance Measures:**

Carrying out measures to shield animals from predation is urgent. This might include the utilization of obstructions like gatekeeper creatures, secure fenced in areas, or even imaginative advancements like blazing lights and sound gadgets to deter hunters from moving toward homegrown creatures.

6. **Preservation Halls:**

Making natural life halls that interface divided environments can work with the development of creatures, decreasing their dependence on human-ruled regions. This keeps up with hereditary variety and permits species to satisfy their biological jobs while limiting struggles with human exercises.

7. **Strategy and Legitimate Systems:**

Vigorous arrangements and legitimate structures are fundamental for tending to human-untamed life clashes at both nearby and public levels. This incorporates regulation that upholds preservation endeavors, manages land use, and addresses pay systems for misfortunes caused by networks because of natural life collaborations.

V. Contextual analyses in Human-Untamed life Peace making

1. **Elephant Halls in India:**

In India, where elephants frequently clash with human settlements, endeavors have been made to lay out elephant hallways. These safeguarded pathways permit elephants to move between divided environments, diminishing experiences with people and limiting struggles.

2. **Domesticated animals Watchman Canines in Africa:**

In pieces of Africa, especially where huge carnivores compromise domesticated animals, the utilization of domesticated animals gatekeeper canines has demonstrated compelling. These extraordinarily prepared canines assist with dissuading hunters, lessening examples of domesticated animals plunder and alleviating clashes among pastoralists and natural life.

3. Concurrence Drives in North America:

In North America, drives, for example, the Yellowstone to Yukon Protection Drive center around keeping up with natural life passageways to consider the free development of species like wild bears and wolves. Through training and local area commitment, these drives expect to cultivate conjunction among untamed life and nearby populaces.

VI. Difficulties and Future Headings

While huge steps have been made in understanding and alleviating human-untamed life clashes, various difficulties persevere. Quick urbanization, worldwide environmental change, and political precariousness keep on worsening these struggles. Additionally, financing requirements, restricted assets, and changing levels of human-natural life struggle mindfulness present continuous difficulties for viable protection procedures.

The fate of human-natural life peace making lies in interdisciplinary exploration, imaginative advances, and versatile protection techniques. By tending to the main drivers of contentions and executing extensive, local area driven arrangements, moderates can endeavor towards a more agreeable concurrence among people and untamed life.

7.1 Challenges of Coexistence with Rhinos

Existing together with rhinos presents a remarkable arrangement of difficulties that require a sensitive harmony between human necessities and the safeguarding of these notable species. While rhinos are fundamental for keeping up with biodiversity and natural equilibrium, their presence can present difficulties for nearby networks and progressives. This exposition dives into the complex difficulties related with coinciding with rhinos, investigating issues connected with natural surroundings misfortune, human-untamed life struggle, poaching, and the financial ramifications of protection endeavors.

II. Territory Misfortune and Fracture

1. **Agrarian Development:**
   One of the essential difficulties in coinciding with rhinos is territory misfortune because of agrarian development. As human populaces develop, the interest for arable land builds, prompting the change of regular natural surroundings into agrarian fields.

   This infringement into rhino natural surroundings brings about territory discontinuity and disengagement, upsetting conventional movement courses and restricting the accessible space for rhinos.

2. **Urbanization and Foundation Advancement:**

Urbanization and foundation advancement further compound living space misfortune. Streets, parkways, and other development projects part rhino environments, disengaging populaces and upsetting their capacity to uninhibitedly move. The infringement of human settlements into rhino domains represents a danger not exclusively to the rhinos yet additionally improves the probability of human-untamed life clashes.

III. Human-Natural life Struggle

1. **Crop Assaulting:**
   Human-natural life struggle is a huge test in regions where rhinos and human networks share scenes. Rhinos, especially the white rhinoceros, are known to take part in crop assaulting. These occurrences bring about financial misfortunes for ranchers, prompting retaliatory measures against the rhinos and raising clash between the two gatherings.

2. **Domesticated animals Ravaging:**
   Notwithstanding crop assaulting, rhinos might cause clashes by pillaging animals. However rhinos are essentially herbivores, their size and developments can unintentionally prompt harm to walls or damage to homegrown creatures. This can bring about monetary misfortunes for neighborhood networks, prompting negative view of rhinos and expanding the potential for struggle.

3. **Human Wellbeing Concerns:**

Rhinos, particularly when they feel compromised or cornered, can represent an immediate danger to human security. Experiences among rhinos and individuals, especially in regions where human populaces are thick, may bring about wounds or fatalities. This makes dread and hostility towards rhinos, entangling preservation endeavors.

IV. Poaching for Rhino Horns

1. **Unlawful Natural life Exchange:**
   Perhaps of the most basic test confronting rhino preservation is poaching for their horns. Rhino horns, erroneously accepted to have therapeutic properties, are exceptionally desired in specific societies, driving a worthwhile unlawful untamed life exchange. Poaching seriously endangers rhino populaces and subverts preservation endeavors focused on their insurance.

2. **Interest for Rhino Horns:**
   The interest for rhino horns, driven by conventional convictions and an underground market that values them as extravagance merchandise, fills poaching exercises. In spite of worldwide boycotts and protection endeavors, the excessive cost of rhino horns on the underground market keeps on driving poaching, representing a serious danger to rhino populaces universally.

3. Refinement of Poaching Organizations:

Poaching networks have become progressively modern, utilizing cutting edge innovation and strategies to sidestep policing. This incorporates the utilization of robots, night-vision hardware, and efficient crook organizations. The complexity of these tasks presents an imposing test for moderates attempting to shield rhinos from poaching exercises.

V. Financial Effects of Protection Endeavors

1. **Dislodging of Native People group:**
   Preservation endeavors, while critical for rhino assurance, can unintentionally prompt the relocation of native networks. Severe preservation strategies and the foundation of safeguarded regions might bring about the migration of networks that have generally existed together with rhinos. This dislodging can prompt social and monetary disturbances for these networks.

2. **Influence on Jobs:**
   Preservation drives, for example, limitations ashore use and the travel industry guidelines, may affect the vocations of neighborhood networks. For instance, networks that generally depended on feasible asset use might confront limitations that influence their capacity to get pay from regular assets, prompting financial difficulties.

3. **The travel industry Reliance Issues:**

Numerous protection programs center around advancing natural life the travel industry for of producing income for preservation. Nonetheless, overreliance on the travel industry can make weaknesses, particularly when outside elements, for example, political insecurity or wellbeing emergencies influence guest numbers. This reliance can prompt monetary vulnerabilities for protection projects and the networks they mean to help.

VI. Environmental Change and Territory Movements

1. **Adjusted Natural surroundings Appropriateness:**
   Environmental change represents an extra test for rhino protection by adjusting the appropriateness of their living spaces. Changes in temperature, precipitation examples, and vegetation cover can affect the dispersion of appropriate territories for rhinos. This requires versatile procedures to oversee territories actually and guarantee the drawn out endurance of rhino populaces.

2. **Influence on Water Accessibility:**

Rhinos, in the same way as other different species, depend on unambiguous water sources inside their territories. Environmental change can adjust precipitation designs, influencing water accessibility in rhino regions. Changes in water accessibility can prompt expanded rivalry among rhinos and different species or even outcome in clashes with neighborhood networks over shared water assets.

VII. Preservation Systems to Address Difficulties

1. **Local area Based Preservation:**
   Integrating nearby networks into protection drives is urgent for tending to the difficulties of coinciding with rhinos. Local area based preservation draws near, which include neighborhood cooperation in dynamic cycles and the sharing of advantages from protection endeavors, assist with building positive connections among networks and preservation associations.

2. **Training and Mindfulness Projects:**
   Instructing nearby networks about the significance of rhino protection, dissipating fantasies about rhino horns, and bringing issues to light about the environmental jobs of rhinos are fundamental parts of alleviation methodologies. Informed people group are bound to help protection endeavors and effectively add to decreasing human-untamed life clashes.

3. **Elective Livelihoods:**
   Giving elective work choices to networks living in rhino territories can lessen their reliance on normal assets that might draw in clashes. Manageable agribusiness rehearses, eco-accommodating the travel industry drives, and ability advancement projects can add to both protection objectives and the prosperity of nearby networks.

4. **Against Poaching Measures:**
   Improving enemy of poaching endeavors is basic for rhino protection. This remembers financial planning for innovation, preparing officers, and reinforcing policing battle poaching networks really.
   Global cooperation is additionally vital for check the interest for rhino horns and upset unlawful shipping lanes.

5. **Territory Rebuilding and Availability:**
   Reestablishing debased natural surroundings and laying out untamed life halls to interface divided regions are essential for rhino populaces. These drives take into account the regular development of rhinos and backing hereditary variety inside populaces. Rationing environments overall, instead of disengaged patches, is vital for the drawn out reasonability of rhino living spaces.

6. **Versatile Administration Notwithstanding Environmental Change:**

Adjusting protection systems to address the effects of environmental change on rhino natural surroundings is fundamental. This might include environment reclamation, checking changes in vegetation, and carrying out systems to guarantee water accessibility. Cooperative examination between preservationists, environmentalists, and environment researchers is basic for creating versatile administration plans.

7.2 Conservation Initiatives to Mitigate Human-Wildlife Conflict

Human-natural life struggle (HWC) is an industrious test that requests proactive protection drives to relieve the adverse consequences on both human networks and natural life populaces. As human populaces grow and regular living spaces contract, experiences among people and untamed life become more continuous, prompting clashes that endanger the conjunction of both. This exposition investigates different protection drives intended to address and moderate human-natural life struggle, accentuating the significance of creative methodologies, local area commitment, and supportable practices.

II. Understanding the Underlying drivers of Human-Untamed life Struggle

1. **Environment Misfortune and Fracture:**
   Understanding the underlying drivers of human-untamed life struggle is fundamental for creating successful preservation drives. Territory misfortune and fracture, driven by rural extension, urbanization, and foundation improvement, force untamed life into more modest regions, improving the probability of struggles. Protection endeavors should resolve the hidden issue of contracting living spaces to limit human-untamed life associations.

2. **Asset Contest:**
   Untamed life frequently contends with people for restricted assets like food, water, and space. Farming fields draw in herbivores, prompting crop striking, while hunters might target animals.
   Perceiving the opposition for assets is pivotal for planning drives that advance conjunction instead of compounding clashes.

3. **Absence of Mindfulness and Understanding:**
   Mistaken assumptions and absence of mindfulness about untamed life conduct add to clashes. Schooling drives focused on neighborhood networks can disperse legends, bring issues to light about the environmental jobs of untamed life, and encourage a more noteworthy comprehension of concurrence. Informed people group are bound to embrace rehearses that limit clashes.

4. **Environmental Change Effects:**

Environmental change, with its erratic effects on atmospheric conditions and natural surroundings, adds intricacy to human-untamed life clashes. Protection drives need to think about the changing elements of biological systems and foster versatile methodologies to alleviate the impacts of environmental change on both human and untamed life populaces.

III. Protection Drives to Alleviate Human-Natural life Struggle

1. **Local area Based Protection:**
   Local area based protection is a foundation of compelling human-untamed life struggle moderation. Drawing in neighborhood networks in dynamic cycles and guaranteeing they benefit straightforwardly from protection endeavors encourages a feeling of pride and obligation. Income sharing systems, work amazing open doors, and manageable asset use are indispensable parts of local area based preservation.

2. **Instruction and Mindfulness Projects:**
   Instructive drives assume a critical part in diminishing human-untamed life clashes. Mindfulness projects can target schools, nearby networks, and even natural life insurance organizations to scatter data about the way of behaving of neighborhood untamed life, the significance of conjunction, and techniques to limit clashes. Such drives assist with building a culture of resistance and understanding.

3. **Early Admonition Frameworks:**
   Creating and executing early admonition frameworks is fundamental for forestalling clashes. Innovation, for example, sensor-based cautions, can alarm networks about the presence of untamed life in nearness. This gives an open door to networks to go to preventive lengths, decreasing the probability of conflicts.

4. **Elective Jobs:**
   Giving elective job choices to networks living in regions inclined to human-untamed life clashes can lessen their reliance on assets that draw in untamed life. Drives might incorporate advancing maintainable farming works on, creating eco-accommodating the travel industry, and working with elective pay sources that limit collaborations with natural life.

5. **Fencing and Boundary Drives:**
   Actual boundaries like fences and channels can be successful in keeping natural life from entering human settlements or rural fields. Key situation of obstructions and the utilization of innovation, for example, sensor-initiated impediments, can essentially decrease the occurrence of harvest assaulting or domesticated animals plunder.

6. **Animals Security Measures:**
   In locales where carnivores represent a danger to domesticated animals, carrying out measures to safeguard animals can assist with diminishing struggles. This might include the utilization of gatekeeper creatures, secure walled in areas, and, surprisingly, imaginative advancements like blazing lights and sound gadgets to deter hunters from moving toward homegrown creatures.

7. **Preservation Passageways:**
   Making protection passages that associate divided natural surroundings empowers untamed life to move openly across scenes. This decreases the tension on neighborhood natural surroundings and limits clashes emerging from confined

development. Preservation hallways are urgent for keeping up with hereditary variety and environmental equilibrium.

8. **Compromise Groups:**
Laying out specific compromise groups can assume an essential part in overseeing and moderating contentions. These groups, containing prepared people with skill in both untamed life conduct and compromise, can answer quickly to struggle circumstances, executing estimates that focus on security for the two people and untamed life.

9. **Remuneration and Protection Projects:**
Remuneration programs that repay networks for misfortunes caused because of untamed life connections can assist with building altruism and backing for preservation drives. Also, protection programs that give inclusion to edit harm or domesticated animals misfortunes because of untamed life can ease the financial weight on impacted networks.

10. **Global Cooperation:**

Human-natural life clashes frequently rise above public boundaries. Cooperative endeavors between nations, worldwide associations, and non-administrative substances are urgent for creating thorough techniques. Sharing information, assets, and best practices guarantees a brought together way to deal with moderating human-untamed life clashes on a worldwide scale.

IV. Contextual analyses in Fruitful Human-Natural life Struggle Relief

1. **Living with Lions in Kenya:**
In specific districts of Kenya, where lions frequently collide with neighborhood networks, the "Lion Watchmen" program has been effective. This people group based drive utilizes neighborhood Maasai heroes to screen and safeguard lion populaces. The champions go about as ministers, alleviating clashes by advancing concurrence and executing early admonition frameworks.

2. **Elephant-Accommodating Tea in India:**
In India, where human-elephant clashes are predominant, the Elephant Family association has presented the idea of "Elephant-Accommodating Tea." This drive urges tea ranches to take on untamed life agreeable practices, for example, keeping up with elephant hallways and trying not to establish crops that draw in elephants. By incorporating protection into tea creation, the drive diminishes clashes and supports nearby networks.

3. **Untamed life Well disposed Beekeeping in Nepal:**

In Nepal, clashes between Himalayan bears and networks have been moderated through untamed life amicable beekeeping. Bee colony walls are introduced around agrarian fields, stopping bears from entering. The drive safeguards crops as well as gives an extra kind of revenue for networks through the offer of honey.

V. Difficulties and Future Bearings

While various protection drives show guarantee in moderating human-natural life clashes, challenges persevere. Finding some kind of harmony between preservation objectives and the necessities of nearby networks requires continuous variation and advancement. Subsidizing limitations, political insecurity, and varying points of view on natural life protection present difficulties that should be tended to cooperatively.

Future bearings in human-untamed life struggle relief include embracing state of the art advances, refining local area commitment methodologies, and integrating environmental change contemplations into preservation arranging. Versatile administration, which includes nonstop checking and change of protection methodologies in view of criticism and evolving conditions, is essential for long haul achievement.

7.3 Success Stories and Lessons Learned

Protection drives overall have yielded the two victories and examples that shape the eventual fate of ecological stewardship. Examples of overcoming adversity exhibit the versatility of biological systems, the recuperation of jeopardized species, and the positive effects on neighborhood networks. Nonetheless, these accomplishments come inseparably with important examples that highlight the intricacy of protection work. This article investigates remarkable examples of overcoming adversity and the illustrations gained from different protection drives, giving bits of knowledge into powerful techniques, challenges confronted, and the advancing scene of preservation endeavors.

II. Examples of overcoming adversity in Protection

1. **Bald Eagle Recuperation in the US:**

   The recuperation of the bald eagle (Haliaeetus leucocephalus) in the US remains as a milestone example of overcoming adversity. When near the precarious edge of termination because of territory misfortune, pesticide openness (explicitly DDT), and unlawful hunting, coordinated protection endeavors prompted the restricting of DDT in 1972. Ensuing natural surroundings security, hostage rearing projects, and public mindfulness crusades added to the bald eagle's expulsion from the imperiled species list in 2007. Today, the bald eagle populace flourishes across the US.

2. **Goliath Panda Preservation in China:**

   China's goliath panda (Ailuropoda melanoleuca) preservation program is praised worldwide. Confronted with environment discontinuity and a declining populace, China carried out measures, for example, laying out safeguarded saves, reforestation drives, and hostage reproducing programs. The fruitful renewed introduction of pandas into the wild, alongside supported populace development, exhibits the adequacy of incorporated protection techniques. The goliath panda's status was redesigned from "imperiled" to "powerless" in 2016.

3. **Galápagos Turtle Preservation:**
The Galápagos Islands have seen fruitful preservation endeavors coordinated at the famous monster turtles. Obtrusive species and territory obliteration undermined these exceptional reptiles, however thorough preservation measures, including natural surroundings rebuilding, hostage reproducing, and intrusive species control, have prompted populace recuperations. The goliath turtles of the Galápagos stand as a demonstration of the versatility of environments when upheld by designated preservation activities.

4. **Dark Wolf Renewed introduction in Yellowstone Public Park:**
The renewed introduction of dim wolves (Canis lupus) to Yellowstone Public Park during the 1990s is a prominent progress in North American untamed life protection. In the wake of being extirpated from the recreation area during the 1920s, the renewed introduction meant to reestablish biological equilibrium by controlling elk populaces. The wolves' return had flowing consequences for the biological system, affecting vegetation, streambank soundness, and, surprisingly, the way of behaving of different species. This achievement highlights the significance of cornerstone species in keeping up with biological system wellbeing.

5. **Local area Based Protection in Namibia:**

Namibia's way to deal with local area based preservation has shown striking outcome in safeguarding natural life and enabling neighborhood networks. By conceding common conservancies the privileges to oversee and profit from untamed life assets, Namibia has boosted protection. Untamed life populaces, including elephants and dark rhinos, have bounced back, and networks have encountered financial advantages through the travel industry and manageable asset use. This model exhibits the potential for adjusting protection objectives to local area interests.

III. Examples Gained from Preservation Drives

1. **Coordinated Approaches are Vital:**
Examples of overcoming adversity frequently rise out of incorporated approaches that address various features of protection. Consolidating environment insurance, hostile to poaching measures, local area commitment, and logical examination thinks up an extensive technique. The examples learned underline the interconnectedness of environmental, social, and monetary elements in fruitful preservation drives.

2. **Versatile Administration is Critical:**
Protection is a versatile cycle that requires nonstop learning and change. Fruitful drives consolidate versatile administration, wherein preservation methodologies are refined in view of checking and assessment. Perceiving the powerful idea

of biological systems and being receptive to new data improves the viability of preservation endeavors.

3. **Consideration of Nearby People group:**
   Connecting with nearby networks is basic for fruitful preservation. Projects that consolidate neighborhood information, address local area needs, and give unmistakable advantages make a feeling of responsibility and backing. On the other hand, drives that dismissal or distance neighborhood networks might confront obstruction and difficulties in accomplishing their preservation targets.

4. **Maintainable Vocations are Focal:**
   Protection drives should consider the financial prosperity of neighborhood networks. Reasonable vocations, frequently connected to ecotourism or manageable asset use, can reduce neediness and construct support for preservation. Offsetting ecological assurance with the necessities of networks guarantees long haul achievement.

5. **Political Will and Strategy Backing Matter:**
   Political responsibility and strong arrangements are basic for the outcome of preservation drives. State run administrations that focus on ecological insurance, sanction and implement protection regulations, and dispense assets to preservation endeavors establish an empowering climate for progress. On the other hand, an absence of political will can frustrate progress.

6. **Worldwide Joint effort is Fundamental:**
   Preservation challenges frequently rise above public lines. Examples of overcoming adversity feature the significance of global cooperation, information sharing, and joint endeavors. Shows, deals, and associations work with the trading of aptitude and assets, adding to the worldwide preservation plan.

7. **Science-Based Navigation:**
   Logical examination assumes a key part in viable preservation. Illustrations learned highlight the significance of powerful information assortment, observing, and logical examination to illuminate direction. Proof based preservation procedures upgrade the probability of achievement and manageability.

8. **Public Mindfulness and Support:**
   Public mindfulness and support are incredible assets for protection. Fruitful drives frequently influence public help through training, media missions, and local area contribution. Building a voting demographic that qualities and supports preservation adds to the life span of drives.

9. **Moderating Human-Natural life Struggle is Perplexing:**
   Human-natural life struggle is a multi-layered challenge requiring nuanced approaches. Illustrations from fruitful drives stress the requirement for procedures that consider the main drivers, include nearby networks, and utilize a blend of preventive measures. Tending to human-natural life struggle is significant for cultivating concurrence.

10. **Long haul Responsibility is Fundamental:**

Preservation achievement frequently requires long haul responsibility and supported endeavors. Environments and species recuperation take time, and the effects of preservation drives may not be quickly obvious. Diligence and devotion are fundamental for accomplishing enduring outcomes.

IV. Challenges Looked by Preservation Drives

1. **Asset Constraints:**
   Numerous preservation drives face asset requirements, including subsidizing, labor, and innovation. Restricted assets can obstruct the scale and adequacy of drives, making it trying to address the extent of preservation needs.

2. **Political Unsteadiness:**
   Political unsteadiness in specific locales can sabotage protection endeavors. Changes in government, absence of political will, and clashes can disturb progressing drives and frustrate the foundation of strong approaches.

3. **Environmental Change Effects:**
   Environmental change presents difficulties to protection by modifying biological systems, influencing species' living spaces, and influencing movement designs. Protection techniques should be versatile to the changing environment to guarantee their proceeded with pertinence.

4. **Intrusive Species and Illnesses:**
   Intrusive species and illnesses present continuous dangers to biodiversity. Protection drives should fight with the spread of intrusive species and arising illnesses that can disturb environments and effect the progress of renewed introduction or restoration programs.

5. **Absence of Public Help:**

Public help is urgent for the progress of preservation drives. Absence of mindfulness, apathy, or resistance from neighborhood networks or more extensive society can frustrate the execution and supportability of preservation endeavors.

V. Future Bearings in Preservation

1. **Innovation and Advancement:**
   The joining of innovation, including satellite observing, man-made brainpower, and DNA examination, holds guarantee for improving preservation endeavors. Advancements in information assortment, examination, and reconnaissance add to more viable and productive preservation procedures.

2. **Nature-Based Arrangements:**
   Nature-based arrangements, like reforestation, living space rebuilding, and practical land the executives, are acquiring conspicuousness. These methodologies

influence the force of biological systems to address ecological difficulties, including environmental change relief and biodiversity protection.

3. **Green Money and Manageable Speculations:**

The job of green money and reasonable ventures is filling in supporting protection drives. By adjusting monetary assets to protection objectives, drives can get subsidizing for long haul projects and advance earth feasible practices.

4. **Native Information and Customary Practices:**

Perceiving and integrating native information and customary practices into protection drives improves their social pertinence and adequacy. Native people group frequently have significant bits of knowledge into supportable asset the board and biodiversity protection.

5. **Protection Strategy Backing:**

Backing for vigorous preservation arrangements at nearby, public, and global levels is fundamental. Preservation associations and partners should effectively participate in strategy conversations, advancing regulation that upholds ecological security, untamed life protection, and economical turn of events.

6. **Limit Building and Preparing:**

Putting resources into limit building and preparing programs for preservation professionals, nearby networks, and policymakers reinforces the general viability of protection drives. Building nearby aptitude encourages independence and guarantees the drawn out manageability of preservation endeavors.

Chapter 8

Future Perspectives

The fate of preservation presents a unique scene portrayed by a mix of difficulties and valuable open doors. As we look forward, the basic to safeguard biodiversity, address environmental change, and advance maintainable practices turns out to be progressively basic. This article investigates future viewpoints in preservation, looking at arising difficulties, imaginative methodologies, mechanical progressions, and the advancing job of worldwide joint effort in molding the direction of ecological stewardship.

II. Arising Difficulties in Preservation

1. **Environmental Change and Living space Disturbance:**
   The effect of environmental change on biological systems represents a huge test for traditionalists. Changing temperature designs, adjusted precipitation systems, and outrageous climate occasions can upset natural surroundings and movement designs, undermining the endurance of various species. Protection endeavors should adjust to these movements to shield biodiversity in an evolving environment.

2. **Loss of Biodiversity:**
   The continuous loss of biodiversity is a worldwide concern. Human exercises, including living space annihilation, contamination, and overexploitation of regular assets, add to the decay of species around the world. As environments lose their variety, the versatility of these frameworks decreases, making them more defenseless against aggravations.

3. **Human-Natural life Struggle:**
   Human-untamed life struggle keeps on heightening as human populaces grow and regular territories recoil. Experiences among people and natural life bring about monetary misfortunes, dangers to human security, and retaliatory measures against creatures. Compelling procedures for alleviating human-untamed

life struggle are fundamental for cultivating concurrence and guaranteeing the endurance of assorted species.

4. **Obtrusive Species and Infections:**
The presentation and spread of obtrusive species and infections present continuous dangers to local verdure. Obtrusive species can outcompete or go after local species, disturbing biological systems. Infections, like those influencing creatures of land and water and bats, can have flowing consequences for whole environments.

Overseeing and forestalling the spread of invasives and infections is vital for preservation achievement.

5. **Contamination and Territory Corruption:**

Contamination, including plastic waste, substance toxins, and living space corruption, stays an inescapable test. From seas to timberlands, human-produced poisons corrupt environments and mischief natural life. Alleviating contamination and reestablishing corrupted living spaces are fundamental parts of protection endeavors.

III. Imaginative Methodologies and Amazing open doors in Protection

1. **Innovation and Protection:**
Headways in innovation offer new devices and potential open doors for preservation. Remote detecting, satellite symbolism, and information investigation empower more exact checking of environments. Drones work with elevated overviews and observation, giving important bits of knowledge into hard-to-arrive at regions. Preservationists can use these advancements to further develop information assortment, track untamed life developments, and answer natural changes really.

2. **Hereditary Protection and Strength:**
Hereditary protection systems assume a urgent part in safeguarding biodiversity. Drives, for example, seed banks, cryopreservation of hereditary material, and helped conceptive advancements add to the protection of imperiled species. Keeping up with hereditary variety improves the strength of populaces, empowering them to adjust to changing natural circumstances.

3. **Rewilding and Natural surroundings Rebuilding:**
The idea of rewilding, once again introducing cornerstone species, and reestablishing normal territories has acquired noticeable quality. These drives mean to reproduce working biological systems, advancing biodiversity and environment administrations. Enormous scope environment reclamation projects, like reforestation and wetland rebuilding, add to the recuperation of debased scenes.

4. **Preservation Money and Green Ventures:**
The combination of preservation into monetary and speculation systems is an arising pattern. Preservation finance includes utilizing private and public

ventures for protection projects. Green securities and effect putting channel assets into reasonable drives, offering monetary help for protection endeavors and advancing the reconciliation of natural contemplations into financial navigation.

5. **Local area Based Preservation and Native Information:**
Perceiving the job of nearby networks and native information is basic for effective preservation. Local area based preservation, which includes neighborhood networks in dynamic cycles, guarantees that protection endeavors line up with local area needs and values. Integrating native information contributes important experiences into maintainable asset the executives and biodiversity protection.

6. **Nature-Based Answers for Environmental Change:**
Nature-based arrangements include utilizing environments to address environmental change. Reforestation, reasonable land the board, and the security of normal carbon sinks, like mangroves and peatlands, add to environmental change alleviation. Coordinating nature-based arrangements into environment activity procedures upgrades the general adequacy of worldwide endeavors to battle environmental change.

7. **Preservation Innovation for Checking and Requirement:**

Innovation driven arrangements, including man-made consciousness, AI, and sensor organizations, are altering preservation observing and implementation. These devices help in the distinguishing proof of poaching exercises, observing natural life populaces, and surveying the soundness of environments. Shrewd innovation helps with making continuous information streams, taking into account more proactive preservation mediations.

IV. The Developing Job of Worldwide Joint effort

1. **Global Protection Shows and Settlements:**
Worldwide joint effort through global shows and deals stays essential for tending to protection challenges. Arrangements like the Show on Natural Variety (CBD) and the Paris Settlement on environmental change give systems to aggregate activity. Reinforcing and growing such arrangements is critical for organizing endeavors across borders.

2. **Cross-Sectoral Organizations:**
Protection drives progressively include joint effort with different areas, including business, the scholarly world, and common society. Cross-sectoral associations unite alternate points of view, aptitude, and assets to address complex protection challenges. Drawing in with the confidential area encourages supportable strategic policies and adjusts financial interests to protection objectives.

3. **Resident Science and Public Commitment:**
Resident science drives engage people to add to protection endeavors through information assortment, observing, and support. Public commitment and mindfulness crusades bring issues to light about protection issues, cultivating a feeling of obligation and activism. Bridling the aggregate force of residents upgrades the span and effect of protection drives.

4. **Protection Strategy and Backing:**
Protection strategy includes conciliatory endeavors to resolve natural issues at the global level. Taking part in discretionary cycles helps collect political help, impact strategy choices, and activate assets for protection drives. Promotion assumes a vital part in building public and political will for protection activity.

5. **Instruction and Limit Building:**

Putting resources into schooling and limit building is central for building a worldwide local area of protection experts. Preparing projects, studios, and scholarly organizations add to the advancement of talented experts prepared to address arising difficulties. Building protection education among different crowds cultivates a culture of ecological stewardship.

V. Morals and Social Aspects in Preservation

1. **Moral Contemplations in Preservation Practices:**
The moral elements of protection rehearses are acquiring noticeable quality. Inquiries regarding the treatment of individual creatures in imprisonment, the effect of mediations on biological systems, and the thought of creature government assistance in protection choices are basic moral contemplations. Finding some kind of harmony between protection objectives and moral obligations is an advancing test.

2. **Value and Ecological Equity:**
Ecological equity and value are indispensable parts of preservation endeavors. Guaranteeing that protection benefits are dispersed fairly among networks and staying away from adverse consequences on minimized bunches are moral objectives. Perceiving the privileges and information on native networks adds to all the more preservation results.

3. **Comprehensive Preservation Practices:**

Comprehensive preservation rehearses include consolidating assorted viewpoints and voices in dynamic cycles. Drawing in with nearby networks, native gatherings, and underestimated populaces guarantees that protection drives are socially delicate and address the issues, everything being equal. Inclusivity improves the authenticity and adequacy of protection endeavors.

8.1 Emerging Threats to Rhino Populations

Rhinos, magnificent and famous animals, face a variety of dangers that endanger their endurance. Notwithstanding protection endeavors, arising difficulties have increased the predicament of rhino populaces universally. This article digs into the arising dangers to rhinos, breaking down the intricate elements adding to their weakness. By understanding these difficulties, we can foster designated preservation procedures to guarantee the drawn out endurance of rhinoceros species.

II. Verifiable Setting of Rhino Preservation

1. **Verifiable Decay and Protection Endeavors:**
   Rhinos have gotten through a past filled with decline, driven principally by living space misfortune and poaching. By the late twentieth 100 years, a few animal varieties were near the precarious edge of elimination. Preservation drives, including the foundation of safeguarded regions, against poaching measures, and local area commitment, prompted a few victories, with populaces giving indications of recuperation.

2. **Victories and Remaining Difficulties:**

The southern white rhino (Ceratotherium simum) and more prominent one-horned rhino (Rhinoceros unicornis) represent fruitful preservation stories. In any case, the northern white rhino (Ceratotherium simum cottoni) stays nearly elimination, and the dark rhino (Diceros bicornis) faces persevering dangers. In spite of past accomplishments, arising difficulties present new obstacles for rhino preservation.

III. Arising Dangers to Rhino Populaces

1. **Poaching for Conventional Medication:**
   While rhino horn exchange for conventional medication has been a verifiable danger, it proceeds to endure and develop. Request from Asian business sectors, driven by social convictions in the mending properties of rhino horn, fills unlawful poaching. Complex lawbreaker organizations, frequently engaged with transnational coordinated wrongdoing, add to the persevering danger of rhino poaching.

2. **Expanding Request in Unlawful Natural life Exchange:**
   Rhino horn's apparent unique case and worth on the bootleg market make it a rewarding ware. Regardless of global boycotts, unlawful untamed life exchange networks adjust and track down new roads to take advantage of. The interest for rhino horn in elaborate and restorative items adds to the unlawful exchange, coming down on rhino populaces.

3. **Territory Misfortune and Fracture:**
   Territory misfortune, driven by farming extension, foundation improvement, and urbanization, stays a critical danger to rhinos. Fracture of normal living spaces secludes rhino populaces, restricting quality stream and lessening the

accessibility of reasonable environments. As human populaces keep on developing, finding a harmony among improvement and preservation turns out to be progressively difficult.

4. **Environmental Change Effects:**

The impacts of environmental change represent a new and complex test for rhinos. Modified precipitation designs, changing vegetation elements, and expanded recurrence of outrageous climate occasions can disturb rhino natural surroundings. Adjusting to these progressions is vital for the drawn out endurance of rhino populaces, particularly in districts where environment influences are articulated.

5. **Human-Natural life Struggle:**

As human populaces venture into rhino living spaces, clashes among rhinos and nearby networks heighten. Crop assaulting by rhinos prompts financial misfortunes for ranchers, and thusly, retaliatory measures against rhinos further fuel the issue. Adjusting the necessities of the two rhinos and nearby networks becomes basic to guarantee concurrence.

6. **Illness Dangers:**

The possible spread of illnesses, both from homegrown creatures to rhinos and among rhino populaces, represents a developing danger. Sickness episodes can have pulverizing results, influencing rhino wellbeing and conceptive achievement. Tending to illness chances requires proactive administration techniques and cooperative endeavors among traditionalists and veterinarians.

7. **Hereditary Bottlenecks and Inbreeding:**

Little and divided rhino populaces face the gamble of hereditary bottlenecks and inbreeding. Restricted hereditary variety lessens the capacity of populaces to adjust to changing conditions and expands weakness to infections.
Protection techniques should address these hereditary worries to guarantee the drawn out suitability of rhino populaces.

8. **Political Flimsiness and Powerless Policing:**

Rhino preservation frequently converges with districts set apart by political flimsiness, debasement, and powerless policing. These variables establish a climate helpful for criminal operations, including poaching and dealing. Reinforcing administration designs and policing fundamental for successful rhino preservation.

IV. Protection Techniques In light of Arising Dangers

1. **Hostile to Poaching Measures:**

Upgrading against poaching endeavors is basic to controlling the unlawful exchange rhino horn. This remembers effective money management for innovation like robots, satellite reconnaissance, and sensor organizations, as well as preparing and preparing officers to watch and safeguard rhino living spaces. The utilization of knowledge drove methodologies can disturb poaching organizations and destroy criminal associations engaged with the unlawful exchange.

2. **Request Decrease Missions:**
Tending to the main driver of rhino poaching includes lessening the interest for rhino horn. Public mindfulness crusades in buyer nations, especially in Asia, can scatter legends about the restorative properties of rhino horn and feature the preservation ramifications of its exchange. Cooperative endeavors with conventional medication professionals and commitment with nearby networks are vital parts of interest decrease drives.

3. **Environment Insurance and Reclamation:**
Protecting and reestablishing rhino living spaces is key for their drawn out endurance. This incorporates the foundation and support of safeguarded regions, the making of natural life halls to associate divided living spaces, and reforestation endeavors. Moderates should work cooperatively with nearby networks to foster reasonable land-use rehearses that benefit the two people and rhinos.

4. **Environmental Change Transformation Systems:**
Protection systems should integrate environmental change transformation measures to assist rhinos with adapting to moving natural circumstances. This might include living space rebuilding, water asset the executives, and the formation of environment strong scenes. Cooperative examination between environment researchers and preservationists is fundamental for creating viable transformation systems.

5. **Local area Based Preservation:**
Including nearby networks in preservation drives is urgent for tending to human-natural life struggle and advancing conjunction. Local area based preservation draws near, for example, income sharing projects, manageable work activities, and training programs, assemble positive connections among networks and rhino protection endeavors. Engaging nearby networks to become stewards of their regular assets cultivates a feeling of shared liability.

6. **Global Joint effort:**
The transnational idea of the rhino poaching emergency requires global coordinated effort. Cooperative endeavors between nations, protection associations, and policing are fundamental for sharing insight, organizing hostile to poaching tasks, and blending preservation procedures. Joint drives can reinforce the worldwide reaction to rhino protection challenges.

7. **Examination and Observing Projects:**
Putting resources into logical examination and checking programs is fundamental for acquiring experiences into rhino conduct, wellbeing, and populace elements. Cutting edge innovations, for example, GPS following, camera traps, and hereditary investigation, contribute important information for informed

protection independent direction. Nonstop observing takes into account versatile administration methodologies that answer arising dangers.

8. **Hereditary Administration and Reproducing Projects:**
To address hereditary worries, progressives execute painstakingly oversaw reproducing programs. These projects plan to keep up with hereditary variety inside populaces and forestall inbreeding. Coordination between various rhino-holding organizations, both in situ and ex situ, is basic for guaranteeing the hereditary soundness of hostage and wild populaces.

9. **Limit Building and Preparing:**
Building the limit of nearby networks, protection associations, and policing is pivotal for the compelling execution of preservation methodologies. Preparing programs for officers, preservation experts, and local area individuals improve their abilities in enemy of poaching endeavors, natural surroundings the executives, and compromise.

10. **Strategy Backing and Requirement:**

Backing for strong protection approaches, upheld by severe authorization, is fundamental for establishing an empowering climate for rhino preservation.

States and worldwide bodies assume an essential part in sanctioning and executing regulations that discourage poaching, dealing, and environment obliteration. Drawing in with policymakers and supporting for more grounded regulation adds to the general progress of protection endeavors.

8.2 The Role of Climate Change in Rhino Ecosystems

Environmental change represents a diverse test to biological systems around the world, and rhino living spaces are no special case. Rhinos, charming megafauna species, are profoundly interconnected with their surroundings, making them defenseless against the modifications achieved by environmental change. This article investigates the job of environmental change in rhino biological systems, analyzing the immediate and backhanded influences on rhino populaces and their living spaces. Also, it digs into preservation techniques pointed toward alleviating the outcomes of environmental change to guarantee the strength and endurance of rhino biological systems.

II. Environmental Change and Rhino Natural surroundings

1. **Modified Precipitation Examples:**
Environmental change impacts precipitation designs, prompting shifts in precipitation recurrence and force. Rhinos, especially those in prairie territories, depend on unambiguous vegetation types that are exceptionally delicate to changes in water accessibility. Changed precipitation examples can influence the overflow and appropriation of these key plant species, affecting the dietary assets accessible to rhinos.

2. **Temperature Limits:**
Expanding worldwide temperatures add to more continuous and extreme heatwaves. Rhinos, adjusted to explicit temperature ranges, may encounter heat pressure and parchedness during delayed times of raised temperatures. Heat pressure can influence their general wellbeing, generation, and scavenging ways of behaving, representing an immediate danger to rhino populaces.

3. **Changing Vegetation Elements:**
Environmental change impacts vegetation piece and conveyance, which has flowing consequences for rhino natural surroundings. Changes in plant networks might bring about the downfall of favored scavenge species or the infringement of less satisfactory vegetation. Rhinos, as particular slow eaters, rely upon a particular eating regimen, and modifications in vegetation elements can influence their wholesome admission.

4. **Water Shortage and Accessibility:**
Changes in precipitation designs and expanded vanishing because of higher temperatures add to water shortage in specific rhino natural surroundings. Water accessibility is urgent for rhinos for drinking, floundering (a way of behaving significant for thermoregulation and parasite control), and supporting by and large biological system wellbeing. Decreased water accessibility can escalate rivalry among untamed life and increase the gamble of parchedness for rhinos.

5. **Changes in Environment Reasonableness:**

Environmental change-actuated adjustments in temperature and vegetation might bring about shifts in natural surroundings reasonableness for rhinos. Conventional reaches might turn out to be less ideal, driving rhinos to relocate looking for reasonable circumstances. Territory discontinuity and obstructions, for example, human settlements and foundation can prevent these relocation designs, confining populaces and restricting hereditary trade.

III. Direct Effects on Rhino Wellbeing and Conduct

1. **Heat Pressure and Lack of hydration:**
Increasing temperatures and heatwaves present direct dangers to rhino wellbeing. Heat pressure can prompt lack of hydration, influencing their physiological capabilities and expanding weakness to infections. Delayed openness to high temperatures might adjust rhino conduct, influencing taking care of examples, day to day schedules, and conceptive exercises.

2. **Expanded Weakness to Infections:**
Environmental change can make conditions helpful for the multiplication of infections influencing rhinos. Hotter temperatures and changes in precipitation can impact the conveyance and wealth of illness vectors like ticks and

mosquitoes. This, thusly, lifts the gamble of rhinos contracting illnesses, incorporating those with possibly extreme ramifications for populace wellbeing.

3. **Diminished Conceptive Achievement:**
   Environment initiated stressors can influence the regenerative progress of rhinos. Heat pressure and changes in food accessibility might prompt decreased ripeness, lower rates of birth, and expanded calf mortality. These elements on the whole add to difficulties in keeping up with steady and sound rhino populaces.

4. **Disturbance of Searching Way of behaving:**

Changes in vegetation piece and wholesome quality can upset the searching way of behaving of rhinos. The decay of favored scavenge species might drive rhinos to adjust their taking care of propensities or travel longer distances looking for reasonable food. Such interruptions can prompt hunger, influencing by and large wellness and regenerative abilities.

IV. Roundabout Effects on Rhino Biological systems

1. **Changes in Species Cooperations:**
   Environmental change can adjust the collaborations among rhinos and different species in their biological systems. Changes in vegetation might affect the accessibility of nourishment for different herbivores, possibly prompting expanded contest. Moreover, changes in plant networks might influence the overflow of bugs, affecting the eating routine of bug eating species that coincide with rhinos.

2. **Expanded Human-Natural life Struggle:**
   Environment actuated shifts in living space appropriateness and asset accessibility can fuel human-natural life struggle. As rhinos look for appropriate circumstances, they might infringe upon rural terrains or populated regions, prompting clashes with neighborhood networks. Tending to the subsequent strains is critical for both rhino protection and the prosperity of human populaces.

3. **Changed Fire Systems:**
   Environmental change can impact the recurrence and power of rapidly spreading fires, affecting rhino living spaces. Changes in precipitation examples and temperature can add to additional continuous or serious flames, influencing the vegetation construction and piece. Modified fire systems can prompt natural surroundings corruption, diminishing the accessibility of reasonable scavenge for rhinos.

4. **Hereditary Variety and Flexibility:**

The segregation of rhino populaces because of territory discontinuity and changing ecological circumstances might influence their hereditary variety. Decreased quality stream can restrict the versatile capability of populaces, making them more helpless to ecological stressors and less fit for answering developing difficulties.

V. Preservation Systems Even with Environmental Change

1. **Environment The executives and Rebuilding:**
Preservation endeavors should zero in on natural surroundings the executives and reclamation to upgrade the versatility of rhino environments.
This incorporates the ID and assurance of environment versatile living spaces, reclamation of corrupted regions, and the making of untamed life hallways to work with normal developments. Cooperative drives with neighborhood networks are fundamental for carrying out supportable land-use rehearses.

2. **Environment Versatile Scenes:**
Preservation procedures ought to integrate environment strong scene arranging. This includes evaluating the weakness of rhino natural surroundings to environmental change, distinguishing key variation techniques, and executing measures to improve biological system strength. Scene scale preservation arranging can advance availability, work with relocation, and decrease the confinement of rhino populaces.

3. **Water The executives Systems:**
Given the significance of water accessibility for rhinos, it is vital to carry out compelling water the executives techniques. This incorporates the rebuilding and security of water sources, the production of fake water focuses in basic regions, and checking and overseeing water quality. Such measures add to the general wellbeing and prosperity of rhino populaces.

4. **Environment Versatile Scrounging Techniques:**
Protectionists can attempt to comprehend and uphold the versatile rummaging techniques of rhinos because of changing vegetation elements. This might include the ID of elective scrounge species that are versatile to environmental change, advancing the development of favored species, and observing rhino dietary inclinations to illuminate natural surroundings the executives.

5. **Local area Based Environment Versatility:**
Connecting with neighborhood networks in environment strong preservation rehearses is fundamental. Local area put together drives that concentration with respect to practical asset the board, elective occupations, and environmental change training add to the general flexibility of the two biological systems and the networks that rely upon them. Cooperative direction guarantees that nearby information is coordinated into protection procedures.

6. **Environment Informed Protection Strategies:**
Public and global protection arrangements should be educated by environment science. Coordinating environment contemplations into strategy structures guarantees that protection endeavors are versatile and receptive to evolving conditions. State run administrations and preservation associations can team up to

create and carry out approaches that focus on environment versatility in rhino biological systems.

7. **Infection Checking and The board:**

   Given the expanded gamble of sicknesses influencing rhinos in an evolving environment, checking and the board programs are essential. Normal wellbeing evaluations, illness reconnaissance, and examination into sickness elements empower early identification and mediation. Preservationists can team up with veterinary specialists to foster systems for illness anticipation and control.

8. **Versatile Administration and Exploration:**

   Preservation procedures ought to embrace versatile administration moves toward that consider adaptability and responsiveness to evolving conditions. Progressing investigation into the effects of environmental change on rhinos, their living spaces, and related species gives the establishment to informed navigation. Consistent observing and versatile administration guarantee that protection endeavors stay successful and important.

9. **Worldwide Joint effort for Environment Strong Preservation:**

Given the transboundary idea of rhino environments, worldwide cooperation is fundamental. Nations, preservation associations, and scientists should team up to share information, coordinate protection endeavors, and address normal difficulties. Joint drives add to the advancement of thorough, environment strong methodologies for rhino protection.

8.3 Collaborative Efforts for Sustainable Conservation

Preserving biodiversity and normal environments is a mind boggling and complex test that requests cooperative endeavors on a worldwide scale. Notwithstanding natural dangers, for example, territory misfortune, environmental change, and poaching, the significance of encouraging associations among legislatures, non-administrative associations (NGOs), nearby networks, and the confidential area couldn't possibly be more significant. This article investigates the meaning of cooperative endeavors for feasible protection and looks at how organizations can add to compelling and enduring arrangements.

II. The Force of Joint effort in Protection

1. **Shared Assets and Skill:**

   Cooperative protection endeavors unite different partners, each contributing remarkable assets and aptitude. States might give administrative systems and safeguarded regions, NGOs can offer particular information and local area commitment, while the confidential area might contribute subsidizing and imaginative advancements. By pooling assets and ability, cooperative drives make collaborations that intensify the effect of preservation activities.

2. **Utilizing Nearby Information:**
Nearby people group assume a vital part in preservation, as they frequently have private information on their environments. Cooperative endeavors that include networks in dynamic cycles, embrace customary environmental information, and backing economical vocations engage local people to become stewards of their regular assets. This comprehensive methodology upgrades the viability of preservation measures as well as cultivates a feeling of responsibility and responsibility among local area individuals.

3. **Transboundary Preservation:**
Numerous environments and untamed life species rise above public boundaries, underlining the requirement for transboundary coordinated effort. Cooperative drives between adjoining nations work with the making of natural passages, orchestrate preservation strategies, and empower facilitated reactions to shared difficulties. Models incorporate cross-line safeguarded regions and drives that address the transitory examples of untamed life, guaranteeing their endurance across extensive scenes.

4. **Public-Private Associations:**

Connecting with the confidential area in protection endeavors is vital for accomplishing maintainability. Public-private associations (PPPs) can adjust preservation objectives to financial matters, prompting interests in ecologically capable practices. By advancing manageable stock chains, eco-the travel industry drives, and corporate social obligation, these associations add to both preservation and monetary turn of events.

III. Instances of Fruitful Cooperative Protection Endeavors

1. **The Worldwide Tiger Drive:**
The Worldwide Tiger Drive is a commendable cooperation including legislatures, NGOs, and global associations. Sent off in light of the exceptional decrease in tiger populaces, the drive means to twofold tiger numbers by 2022. Through composed endeavors across tiger-range nations, it tends to poaching, territory misfortune, and human-natural life struggle. The association highlights the significance of worldwide collaboration to safeguard imperiled species.

2. **The Incomparable Green Wall Drive:**
The Incomparable Green Wall Drive embodies a mainland wide cooperative work to battle desertification and land corruption in Africa. Extending across the Sahel locale, this drive includes various nations and accomplices with assorted mastery. By establishing a mosaic of trees and vegetation, the undertaking intends to reestablish corrupted land, work on nearby vocations, and improve environment strength.

3. **The Coral Triangle Drive:**

The Coral Triangle, known as the focal point of marine biodiversity, faces dangers, for example, overfishing and environmental change. The Coral Triangle Drive unites six nations to shield this basic marine district. Cooperative activities incorporate the foundation of marine safeguarded regions, economical fisheries the executives, and local area based preservation. By joining countries with shared interests, the drive means to guarantee the drawn out soundness of the Coral Triangle's environments.

IV. Beating Difficulties through Cooperation

1. **Tending to Clashing Interests:**
   Cooperative preservation experiences difficulties emerging from clashing interests among partners. Offsetting preservation objectives with monetary turn of events, land use, and asset extraction requires nuanced discussion and split the difference. Straightforwardness, discourse, and shared dynamic cycles are fundamental for building agreement and tending to clashing needs.

2. **Guaranteeing Value and Inclusivity:**
   Cooperative endeavors should focus on value and inclusivity to try not to propagate power irregular characteristics. It is significant to perceive and regard the freedoms of nearby networks, native gatherings, and underestimated populaces. Comprehensive dynamic cycles guarantee that the advantages of preservation endeavors are circulated evenhandedly and that assorted viewpoints are thought of.

3. **Supporting Long haul Responsibilities:**

Protection challenges are much of the time long haul, requiring supported responsibility from all accomplices. Cooperative drives should lay out systems for long haul subsidizing, progressing research, and versatile administration. Building a common vision and encouraging a feeling of aggregate liability add to the perseverance of cooperative protection endeavors.

* 9 7 8 8 1 9 6 8 3 2 2 3 0 *